THE *BIG BOOK* OF
LOOM MAGIC

THE **BIG BOOK** OF LOOM MAGIC

75 AWESOME DESIGNS FOR AN AMAZING RAINBOW OF PROJECTS

JOHN McCANN, BECKY THOMAS & MONICA SWEENEY
DESIGNS BY NEARY ALGUARD

Sky Pony Press
New York

Sky Pony Press books may be purchased in bulk at special discounts for sales promotion, corporate gifts, fund-raising, or educational purposes. Special editions can also be created to specifications. For details, contact the Special Sales Department, Sky Pony Press, 307 West 36th Street, 11th Floor, New York, NY 10018 or info@skyhorsepublishing.com.

Sky Pony® is a registered trademark of Skyhorse Publishing, Inc.®, a Delaware corporation.

Visit our website at www.skyponypress.com.

10 9 8 7 6 5 4 3 2 1

Manufactured in the China, November 2014
This product conforms to CPSIA 2008

Library of Congress Cataloguing-in-Publication Data is available on file.

ISBN: 978-1-63450-120-0

CONTENTS

ACKNOWLEDGMENTS

We would like to give many thank-yous to Kelsie Besaw, our champion editor, and to everyone at Skyhorse who worked with remarkable speed on this project. Thank you to Bill Wolfsthal, Tony Lyons, and Linda Biagi for putting this project together. Special thanks to Allan Penn, for your great photography and creative coaching, as well as to Holly Schmidt, for keeping us on track and making delicious sandwiches.

Our enormous gratitude goes to Jax Kordes as well as Olivia Sahagian for contributing such wonderful and unique projects to this book. Your ideas made this book extra special!

To all of the wonderful faces of *Loom Magic!*: Thank you Lucy Bartlett, Sally Brunelle, Quisi Cohen, Charlotte Penn, Noah Rotner, and Caleb and Owen Schmidt. This book would not be the same without you!

Our warmest regards go to each of our contributors, who provided us with truly remarkable, fun, and creative projects to include in this book: thank you Alexandria Seda; Amber Wylie of Hobo Cat Creations; Kate Schultz of Izzalicious Designs (www.izzalicious.com); DIY Mommy on Youtube; and www.elegantfashion360.com.

GLOSSARY

Here is a list of some of the terms we use when explaining how to do each project. Getting to know them will help you speed through all these great designs!

hook: The hook is the off-white, hook-shaped utensil that is provided in the packaging of your loom. This is used to move rubber bands from their pegs instead of your fingers.

c-clip: A c-clip, as its name suggests, is a small, clear clip shaped like a "c" that we use to hold rubber bands together. C-clips are often the last step in a project. Some rubber band kits come with s-clips instead; you can use those the same way you use c-clips.

threading: To thread beads onto your project, wrap a thin piece of wire—such as a stripped twist-tie—around a single band. Add the beads onto the wire from the other end, and then slide them onto the band.

Set up your loom square: When all of the columns are evenly set on the loom; no column of pegs is set forward or backward.

offset: When columns in the loom are not square. For example, when the outside columns are set evenly and the middle column is set one peg closer to you.

Making a chain or **"knitting"**: To make a chain for arms or feet, wrap a single band around your hook three or four times so it looks like a knot. Attach a double band to the end of the hook, and slide the knot onto this double band. Move everything back onto the shaft of the hook. Continue this process of adding double bands to the chain until you have the desired length.

  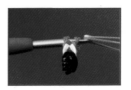 

Holding bands: Holding bands are placed across the rows of your charms before you loop the project. They help to keep all the bands in your designs in the right shape. Do not loop holding bands; when you loop your other bands, pull them through the holding bands as you would with any cap bands.

Doubling: To double a rubber band, fold it onto itself before placing it onto the loom or hook. This makes the band extra tight. When a project calls for doubled bands, the instructions will often say to wrap the band around your hook twice before placing it on the loom; this is an easy way to attach a tight doubled band to multiple pegs. Do not confuse this with a double band: two single bands placed on the loom together.

Double band: Two single rubber bands placed onto the loom together.

How to "Loop" your project back: When you have finished putting down all of your rubber bands on the loom, there is one more step before you can remove your project from the loom. This step connects your bands to each other instead of just to the loom.

To Loop Your Project:

1. Start at the peg indicated in the instructions; usually it is the last or second-to-last peg in your project or the peg where you have put a cap band.

2. Use your plastic hook tool and slide it into the hollow space in the middle of the peg to grab the top un-looped band on the peg.

3. Then pull the band up and off the peg, pulling it through any cap bands or any looped bands stacked above it.

4. Attach the band on your hook to the peg where the other end of the same band is still attached. If there is more than one band, loop all the bands on a peg before you move on to loop the next peg.

5. Pegs are typically looped in the opposite order from how you laid them out on the loom, but be sure to follow any specific instructions for the project you are working on.

6. When you have finished looping your project, you should have a few loose loops remaining on the last peg on the loom. You need to secure those loops by tying a band around them or using a c-clip or your project will unravel!

LOOM
Magic!

OCTO BRACELET

This pattern uses eight bands to make a repeating circle shape: that's why it's called "octo"! Or maybe it's because you'll want to make at least eight bracelets with this fun new stitch!

1. Set up the loom with three rows of pegs, with the middle row set forward one peg (toward you). Loop a rubber band over the middle peg closest to you, then connect it to the peg one up and to the left. Loop another band around this peg and connect it to the peg above it. Loop one band around the peg you ended on, and connect it to the third middle peg. Start at the middle peg closest to you. Loop a band around this peg and connect it to the next peg up and to the right. Finish the rest of the circle as you did with the pegs on the left.

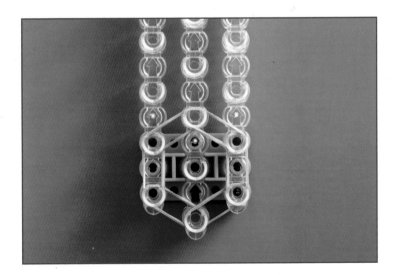

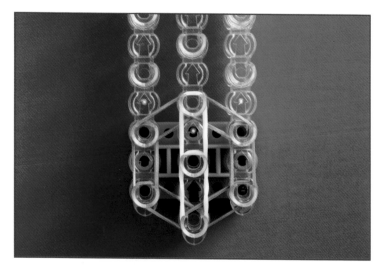

2. Loop a band around the middle peg closest to you, and connect it to the middle peg above it. Repeat with the next peg up.

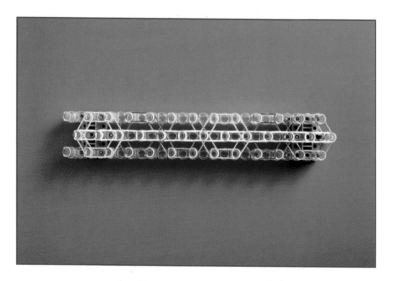

3. Starting on the middle peg three pegs up the loom, repeat steps 2–4, looping the left half of the circle, then the right, then looping the pegs up the middle. Continue up the loom, making 6 total circles. Loop one band around the middle peg furthest from you, then connect it to the peg up and to the right.

4. Turn the loom around so that the arrow is pointing towards you. Starting with the peg closest to you on the right, hook the second loop down on the peg, and pull it up and off the peg, looping it back onto the peg where the other end is still looped. Continue looping the rest of the pegs

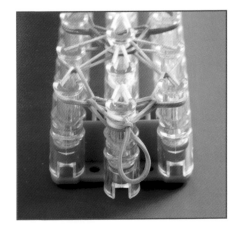

in the same way, working your way up the loom. When you have looped all the rubber bands back onto their starting pegs, turn the loom again so that the arrow is facing away from you, and find the first peg you looped. Use your hook to grab all of the bands on this peg, and loop another band through these bands and pull it tight. You can also use a c-clip for this.

5. Remove the bracelet from the loom. Connect the two ends with a c-clip.

STRAIGHTAWAY BRACELET

This unique design will wow your friends, and it's a breeze to make! It will fit right in with the stack of bracelets on your arm!

You need:

1 loom • hook
36 rubber bands

1. Set up the loom with the red arrow pointing away from you and the middle row set one peg closer to you. Loop a band over the middle peg closest to you, then connect it to the next peg up and to the left. Loop another band over this second peg, and connect it to the peg above. Continue to double loop in this way all the way up the left side of the loom. Do the same on the right side of the loom.

2. Loop one band over the last peg in the row on the left, and connect it to the last peg in the middle row. Do the same with the last peg on the right.

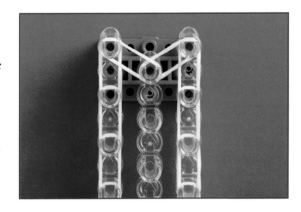

3. Loop a band over the first middle peg, and connect it to the middle peg above it. Loop a band over the closest peg on the left, and connect it to the second middle peg (where you ended your last loop). Loop another band over the closest peg on the right, and connect it to the second middle peg.

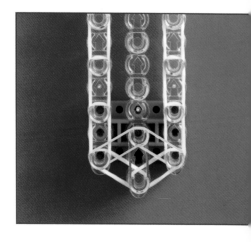

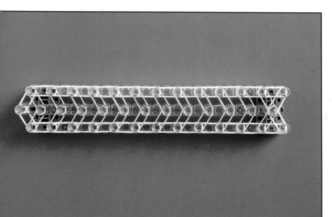

4. Move up to the second middle peg on the loom, and repeat step 3. Continue up the loom in this way until you reach the end.

5. Double-loop a rubber band and put it on the top middle peg.

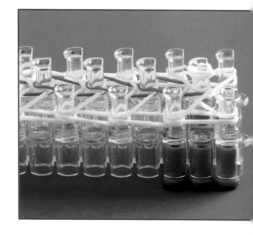

6. Turn the loom around so that the arrow is pointing toward you. Starting with the second middle peg, hook the second band on the peg and pull it up and off, looping back onto the peg where it started. Continue looping up the middle of the loom.

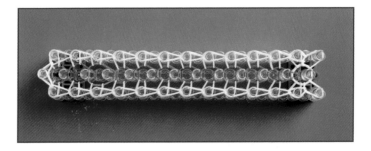

7. Start at the middle peg closest to you. Loop the edges in the same way. Loop the bands off this peg and back onto the first pegs on the left and right. Loop in the same way all the way up the left and right of the loom.

8. Remove your bracelet from the loom.

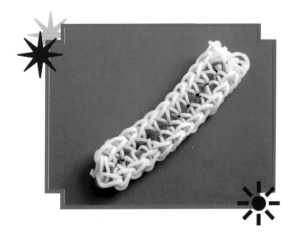

PINNACLE
BRACELET

This pattern is made by repeating a triangle shape all the way up the loom. It comes together quick, and it's sure to be a favorite!

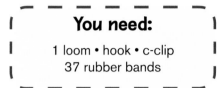

You need:

1 loom • hook • c-clip
37 rubber bands

1. Set up your loom with three rows of pegs set up squarely. Loop a band around the peg closest to you on the right, and connect it to the closest peg on the left (connecting all three pegs in the row). Loop a band around the closest peg on the right, then connect it up to the middle peg in the next row. Do the same with the closest peg on the left.

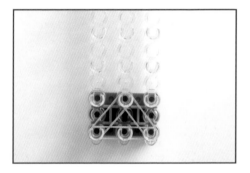

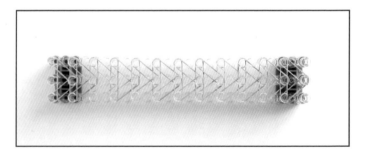

2. Starting on the right peg in the second row, repeat the pattern you made in step 1. Continue until you reach the end of the loom.

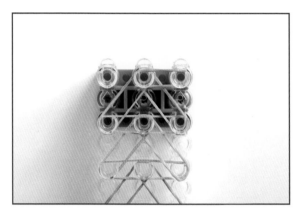

3. Loop a band around the middle peg in the last row, and connect it to the next peg to the right.

4. Turn the loom so the arrow is facing you. Starting with the middle peg, hook the second band from the top and pull it up and off, looping it back to the peg where it started. Move to the next row of pegs, and loop the bands from the corner pegs of the triangle onto the center peg in the same row. Continue looping this way until you've finished the loom.

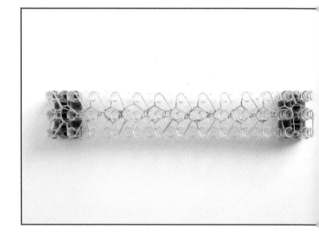

5. Secure the loops from the final peg with a c-clip, and remove your project from the loom.

SQUISHY POOF BALL

This squishy poof ball is so much fun, you won't want to make just one. You can stick these cool little poof balls on your bracelets, your bike handlebars, or the zipper of your backpack, or you can toss them around with your friends! For even more fun, check out the Poof Ball Slingshot on page 27!

You need:

scissors • 1 loom • hook • c-clip
32 rubber bands

1. Set up your loom as shown, with two rows of pegs separated by an empty space between them.

2. Take two rubber bands and tie them together. Repeat until you've used up all but two of the rubber bands.

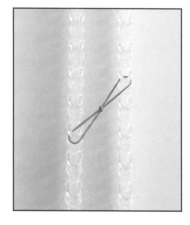

3. Loop one of your tied rubber bands into the loom at an angle.

4. Take another tied rubber band and loop it into the loom at an opposite angle so the knots overlap and the bands make an X shape.

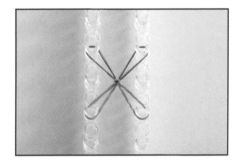

5. Repeat until you've used up all of your tied rubber bands.

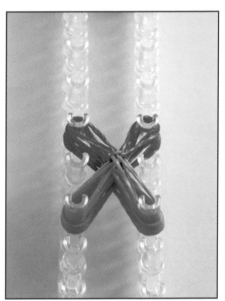

6. Loop one of your leftover rubber bands around your X from top to bottom. Pull one end through the other, and pull it tight.

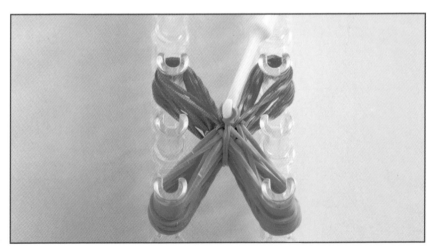

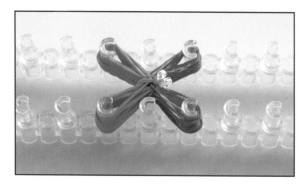

7. Secure the loop with a c-clip.

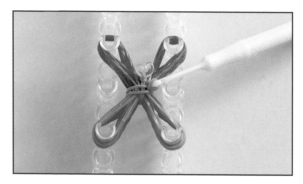

8. Loop your last rubber band around your X in the other direction (right to left), and pull it tight.

9. Hook the loop into the c-clip.

10. Remove your bands from the loom.

11. Cut through the loops at the end of your X. (Be careful not to cut the loops tied around the middle!)

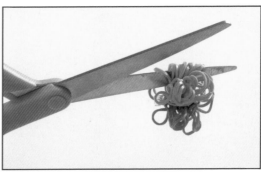

12. Fluff, squish, and squeeze your poof ball to make it round.

Notes: Stack more knotted rubber bands for an even bigger ball! You can also change up your color combinations to make different patterns.

MUSTACHE

Once you make this cool creation, you can twirl your mustache to look just like an evil villain or a video game superhero! Wear it for Halloween, a school play, or when you just feel like goofing around!

You need:
2 looms • 2 c-clips
about 70 rubber bands

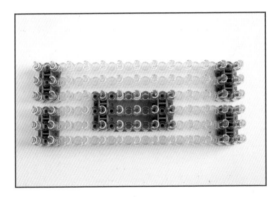

1. Begin with two looms side by side. The pegs should be lined up squarely with the arrows pointing left.

2. Start at the top row all the way to the right. Loop a band around the top right peg, then loop the other end around the peg below it.

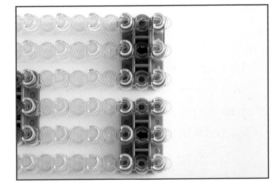

3. Loop a band around the second peg down, and attach it to the peg below, as you did before.

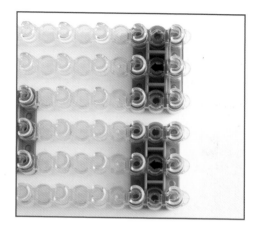

4. Loop another band around the second peg down on the right, and attach this diagonally to the peg one down and to the left. Do the same with the peg just below.

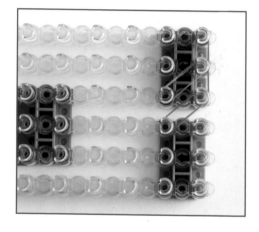

5. Loop a rubber band over the peg where you ended your first diagonal band, then connect it to the peg below, where you ended your second diagonal band.

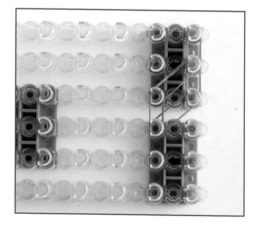

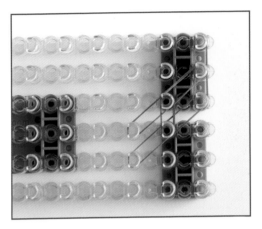

6. Connect a rubber band to the peg where you started your last band, then loop it diagonally to the peg one down and to the left. Do the same starting from the peg below.

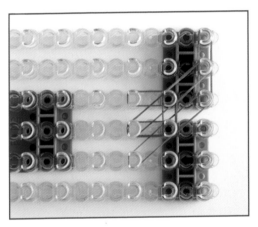

7. Starting at the same peg as the last step, hook a rubber band to connect the peg to the next peg to the left. Do the same with the peg below.

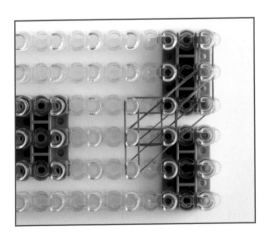

8. Hook a band over the peg where you ended your top horizontal line, then loop the other end over the peg below. Loop a band around the next peg down, and connect it to the peg below.

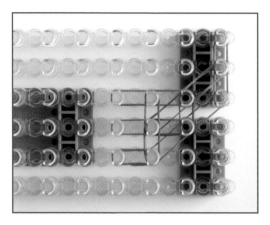

9. On each of the three pegs you connected, loop a rubber band over the peg and connect it to the next peg to the left.

10. Starting again at the top of your connected three pegs, hook a rubber band to the peg and connect it diagonally to the peg below and to the left. Repeat for the next two pegs down.

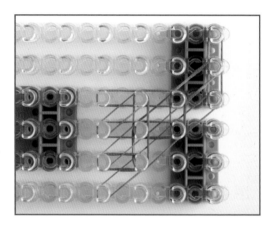

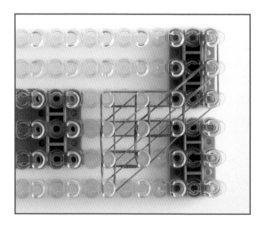

11. Hook a band around the peg on the bottom row where you ended your bottom diagonal loop, and connect it to the peg above it. Repeat with the next two pegs up, connecting four pegs total.

12. On each of the four pegs you just connected, loop a rubber band and connect the peg to the next peg to the left.

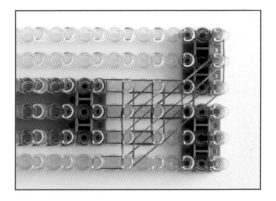

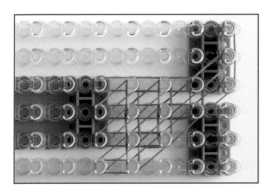

13. Starting at the top of your four connected pegs, loop a rubber band and connect it diagonally to the peg one down and to the left. Do the same for the next two pegs down.

14. From the bottom peg (five from the right), loop a band to connect the peg to the one above it. Repeat for three more pegs, connecting a column of four.

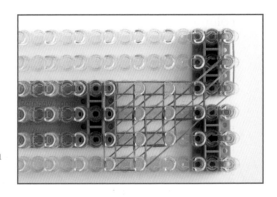

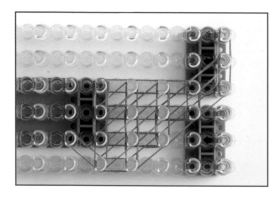

15. From the same bottom peg, attach a rubber band and connect it to the peg up one row and to the left.

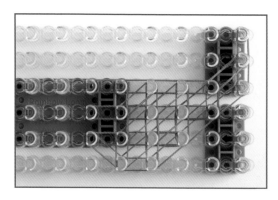

16. Start with the peg just above where you started your last band. Loop a rubber band over the peg and connect it to the peg to the left. Do the same for the next two pegs above the first.

17. Loop a rubber band around the top peg of your four-peg column (five pegs from the left and four from the bottom), and attach the other end diagonally to the peg one down and to the left. Do the same for the next peg down in the column.

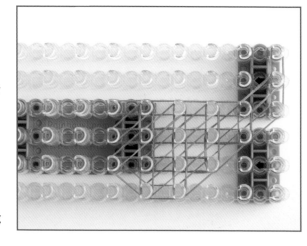

18. Start at the peg where you ended your last diagonal loop (six pegs from the left and one peg away from you). Loop a rubber band over the peg and connect it to the peg above it. Repeat this for the next peg up, making a column of three connected pegs.

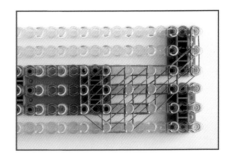

19. Loop a band around the top peg in your three-peg column, and connect the other end diagonally to the peg one down and to the left. Loop a band around the next peg down in the column, and attach it to the same peg to the left. Then loop a third rubber band to the bottom peg in the column, and connect it to the same peg up and to the left.

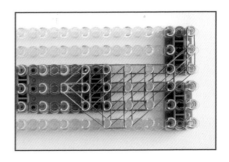

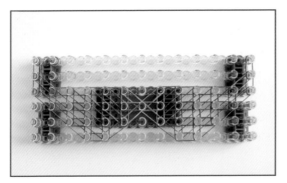

20. To make the other half of the mustache, repeat steps 2 through 19, but lead from the top left peg and move right.

21. When you have finished the other side of the mustache, take another rubber band and wrap it around the center peg three times.

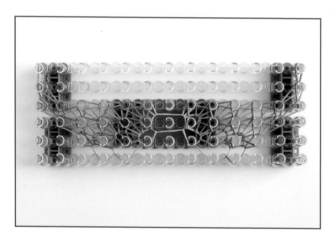

22. Start looping from the center and move outward to each end, pulling the bands off each peg, starting with the band on the bottom, and looping them back to the peg where it started. Loop the lower pegs first, and then work to the top. (This will be different than normal looping as the left side of the mustache will be looped in the opposite direction than normal.)

23. Once the entire mustache has been laid out, place a c-clip on both ends of the mustache.

24. To remove the mustache from the loom, begin pulling from both of the c-clips and work inward toward the center cap band.

Notes: To rock out your 'stache, you can tie a string to each end and wear it around your head. Alternatively, you can try skin-safe adhesive or double-sided sticky tape.

POOF BALL SLiNG SHOT

Ready, aim, fire! This slingshot project is quick and easy—make a bunch with your friends, then line up and see who can shoot the farthest!

You need:

1 loom • hook • c-clip
36 rubber bands

1. Set up the loom with three rows of pegs lined up squarely. Turn the loom so the arrow is facing away from you. Loop a band around the bottom left peg, and connect it to the peg above it. Continue to double loop up the left side of the loom, ending on the fifth peg from you. Do the same on the right side of the loom.

2. Loop a band around the middle fifth peg (right between your columns) and connect it to the peg below and to the left. Loop a second band around the middle peg and connect it to the peg below and to the right. Loop a band to the left peg in the fifth row, then connect it to the center peg in the row. Connect the center peg to the peg on the right.

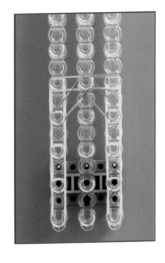

3. Connect the left peg in the fifth row to the peg above it. Do the same on the right side. Loop another band around the fifth peg on the left, and connect to the middle peg in the sixth row, up and to the right. Loop a band around the middle peg in the fifth row, and connect this to the middle peg in the sixth row. Connect the fifth peg on the right in the same way.

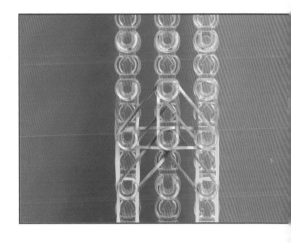

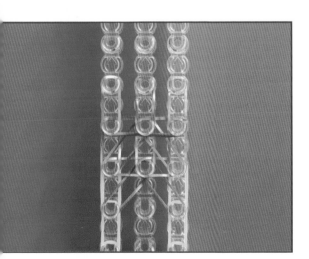

4. Loop a band around the sixth peg on the left and connect it to the middle peg in the row. Connect the middle peg to the peg on the right. Loop another band on the sixth peg on the left, and connect it to the peg above. Connect the middle peg in the sixth row to the peg above it. Connect the sixth peg on the right to the peg above it.

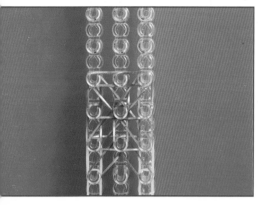

5. Loop a band around the middle peg in the sixth row, and connect it to the next peg up and to the left. Loop another band around the middle peg, and connect it up and to the right. Loop a band over the seventh peg on the left, and connect it to the next peg to the right. Repeat to connect the middle peg to the peg on the right.

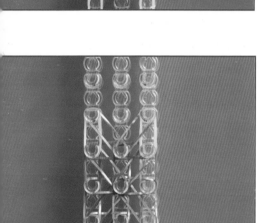

6. Connect the seventh peg on the left to the next peg above it. Do the same on the right side. Loop a band around the middle peg in the seventh row, and connect it to the peg up and to the left. Loop another band around the middle peg and connect it up and to the right.

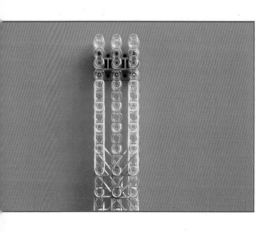

7. Starting on the eighth peg from you on the left, loop a band around the peg, and connect it to the peg above it. Repeat twice more to make a column of three bands. Do the same on the right side of the loom.

8. Turn your loom around so the arrow points toward you. Starting with the fourth peg from you on the left, hook the second band on the peg and pull it up and off, looping it back onto the peg where it started. Do the same with the next three pegs, then repeat on the right. Then loop the diagonal bands in the seventh row back onto the center peg. In the next two rows, loop the diagonal bands onto the center pegs, the horizontal bands from left to right, and then the vertical bands from the bottom to the top. Loop the 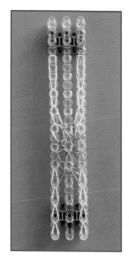 bands on the center peg back to the pegs they came from. Start with the highest non-looped band, then work down until all bands are looped. In this same row, loop the bands on the right and left pegs to the pegs above them. From the center peg in the next row, loop all non-looped bands back to the peg they started on. Starting on the right and left in this same row, loop the bands back up to the peg above it. Continue looping the right and left columns in the same way until you reach the other end of the loom.

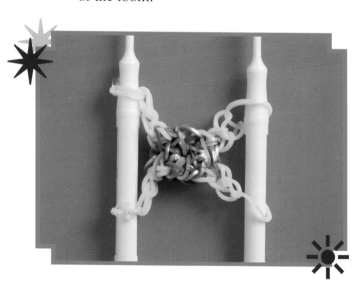

9. Remove your sling shot from the loom.

WATCH BAND

Who wears a watch anymore? You do, with this cool watch band project!

You need:

watch face • 1 loom • hook • c-clip
enough rubber bands for 2 bracelets

1. Set up your loom with the arrow pointing away from you.

2. Hook your favorite pattern onto the loom. We've used the straightaway pattern in our example. If your pattern has a cap band or an extra band at the end to hold it together, skip that step. Do not loop your project yet.

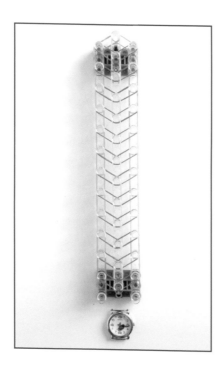

3. Turn the loom so the arrow is pointing toward you.

4. Take the bands at the beginning of the loom (the bands that were placed down last), thread them through the strap bars on the watch face, and loop them back to where they started.

5. Loop the rest of your loom following the directions for the pattern you used.

6. Attach a c-clip to the end, and remove the band from the loom.

7. Repeat steps 2 through 5 to make the other half of the watch band.

8. At the end of the second half of the watch band, run a rubber band through all the final loops and loop it back onto itself (like a lanyard knot). Remove it from the loom.

9. Hook the band to the c-clip, and enjoy your new watch!

DAISY CHAIN BRACELET

Add a little flower power to your loom magic! Create a delightful bracelet with a bouquet of your favorite flowers to wear on your wrist or ankle or even to loop as a key chain. This lovely daisy design is fashionable and fun for any occasion!

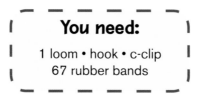

You need:

1 loom • hook • c-clip
67 rubber bands

1. Set up your loom with the middle pegs pulled one closer to you and the arrow pointing away from you. Loop a band around the first middle peg and connect it to the peg above it. Starting at the second middle peg, loop your bands to the left to make the first half of a hexagon, finishing on the fourth middle peg. Start again on the second middle peg, and loop your bands to the right in the same way to finish off your hexagon.

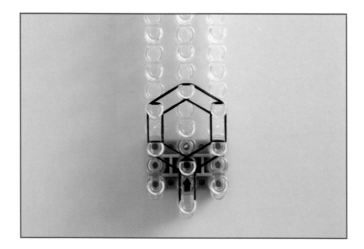

2. To make your "petals," loop a band
   around the third middle peg (in
   the center of your hexagon), and
   connect it to the peg up and to the
   right. Loop another band around the
   middle peg, and connect it to the peg
   down and to the right. Continue to
   connect all six of the outer pegs in
   this way, moving clockwise around
   the hexagon.

3. Triple-loop a
   band, and put it
   on the middle
   peg of your
   hexagon.

4. Starting on the last
   middle peg of your
   hexagon, repeat your
   pattern: loop both sides of
   a new hexagon, then add
   the bands from the center,
   and finish with a triple-

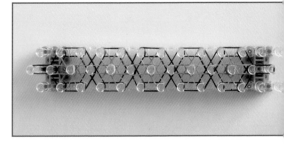

looped cap band on the middle peg. Repeat this up the loom
until you have five hexagons total. On the final hexagon, before
you lay down your bands, loop a band around the last middle
peg in the pattern and connect it to the last peg in the middle
row, then complete the final flower pattern.

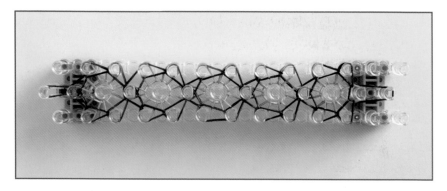

5. Turn the loom around so the arrow is facing toward you. Start looping the bands of your "petals" back onto the pegs where they started: First, loop the bands from the center of the hexagon, starting with the first band under the cap band, then loop counterclockwise around your hexagon. Next, loop the bands that make up the hexagon, starting from the left half and then the right in the same way you placed the bands there in the very first step. Loop all of the "flowers" this way, making your way to the end of the loom.

6. Loop the last band back to the last remaining peg. Attach a c-clip to secure the last band, and then remove your project from the loom.

7. For added length, loop more rubber bands through the end bands before attaching the c-clip.

RAiNBOW CHARM

This rainbow charm will brighten up your day! Whether you hang it from a window, glue it to a refrigerator magnet, or just have it as a keepsake, this eye-popping rainbow is sure to add a little color to your day—rain or shine!

You need:

2 looms • hook • c-clip • 13 PURPLE
26 BLUE • 26 GREEN • 26 YELLOW • 26 ORANGE
and 27 RED rubber bands

1. Set up your two looms side by side with the arrows pointing right.

2. Starting at the bottom left-hand corner, double-loop an entire row of purple bands across the bottom row of the loom. To "double-loop," twist the band onto itself to create a double rubber band before stretching it onto the loom.

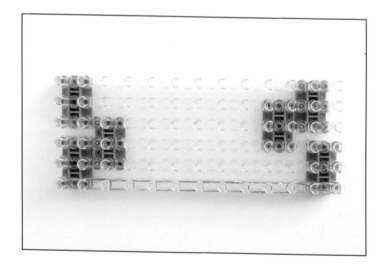

3. Loop a blue band around the peg in the bottom left corner, and then attach it to the next peg above. Do the same with the rest of the pegs in the first row.

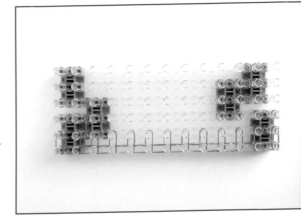

4. In the second row, attach a blue band to the peg all the way to the left, and then connect it to the next peg to the right. Continue looping from left to right until you reach the end of the row.

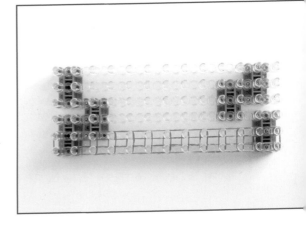

5. Repeat steps 3 and 4, first with green bands, then yellow, orange, and finally red.

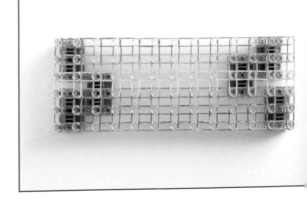

6. Triple-loop a band and put it onto the peg on the top right.

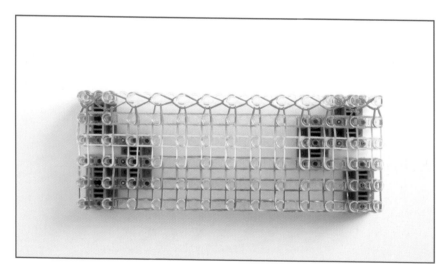

7. Begin looping your project by hooking the second band on the peg and pulling it up and off, then looping it back onto the peg where it started. First loop the top row from right to left, and then loop the vertical bands.

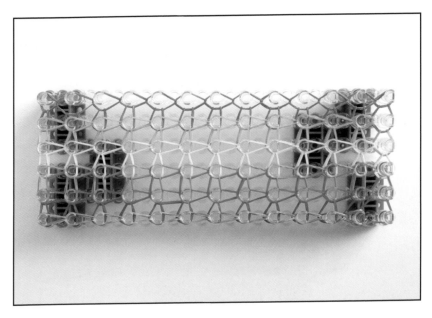

8. Repeat this process for each row.

9. Attach a c-clip to the band on the lower left.

10. Remove your completed project from your loom and see the beautiful rainbow!

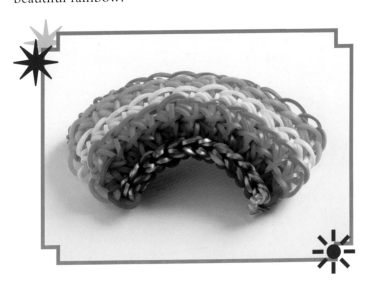

MATCHING BARRETTES

This pattern is a lot like the Octo-Bracelet pattern, but this time there are beads and barrettes to add a little extra fun! Make a matching set and wear them both, or give one to a friend!

You need:

1 loom • hook • 6 pony beads
2 craft barrettes • 25 rubber bands

1. Set up the loom with the middle pegs pulled one closer to you and the arrow pointing away from you. Loop a rubber band over the first middle peg, and then connect it to the peg up and to the left. Loop another band around this peg and connect it to the peg above it. Loop one band around the peg you ended on, and connect it to the third middle peg. Start at the middle peg closest to you and loop the right side of the circle in the same way.

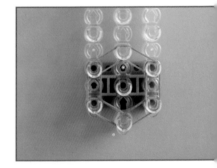

2. Thread a band through one of your beads. Hook one end of the band over the closest middle peg and the other around the middle peg of the circle. Thread a band through another bead, and connect the middle peg to the next peg in the row.

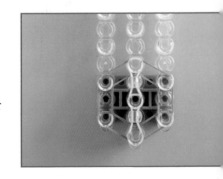

3. Repeat your circle pattern twice more, starting your new circle on the middle peg where you ended your last one, and adding the two beaded bands across the middle row like before. You should have three circles on your loom.

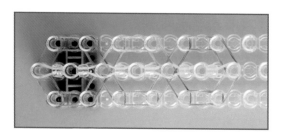

4. Hook a band around the last middle peg of your last circle and connect it to the peg above it.

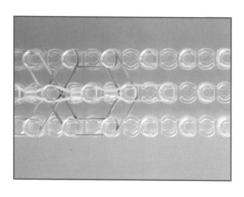

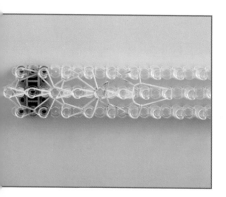

5. Turn the loom around so the arrow is pointing toward you. Starting at the top of your circle, hook the second band on the peg, pull it up and off the peg, and loop it back onto the peg where it began. Continue until all the bands on the peg are unlooped, and then continue looping the rest of the loom, moving toward the end until you have unlooped all the pegs.

6. Take a band and carefully loop it around the bands remaining on the last peg on the loom. Thread the band through its loop (like a lanyard hitch) and pull it tight. Pull it off the loom.

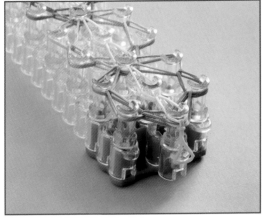

7. Thread one of your end bands through the metal hole of your barrette, and then pull the loop over the rest of the project to secure it. Thread the other end band through the other hole and tie it tightly.

8. Repeat for the other barrette.

CELL PHONE CASE

Dress up your phone with your own custom-made case! This project stretches to fit, so you do not have to worry about measuring. Try out different color combinations and patterns; you can even make a different case for every day of the week!

1. Connect your four looms side by side with the pegs lined up square and the arrows pointing away from you.

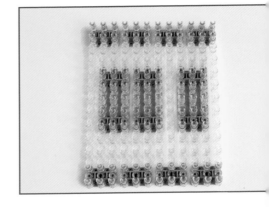

2. Loop a band around one of the middle pegs in the row closest to you, and connect it to the peg right above it.

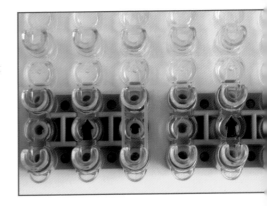

3. Double-loop a rubber band around the peg where you ended your last band, and connect it to the peg to the right. Continue to double-loop to the right for five total pegs, ending on the second to last peg on the right. Then start again at the second middle peg, and loop five more bands in the same way, moving to the left and ending on the last peg in the row.

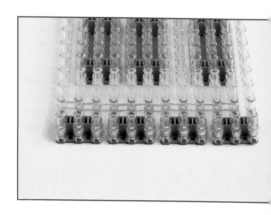

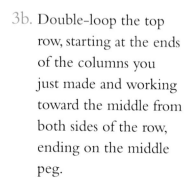

3a. Starting on the corner pegs where you ended your last row, double-loop all the way to the top of the loom on both sides.

3b. Double-loop the top row, starting at the ends of the columns you just made and working toward the middle from both sides of the row, ending on the middle peg.

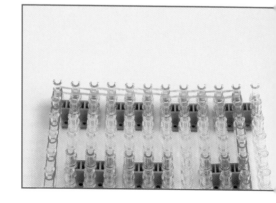

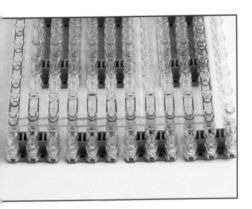

4. Loop a band on the second peg in the second row of your loom, and connect it to the peg above it. Repeat this for the rest of the pegs in the second row, ending on the peg before the right side of your rectangle.

5. Loop a rubber band around the third middle peg, then around the next peg to the right. Repeat for five total pegs. Start again at the third middle peg, and loop five more bands in the same way, moving to the left and ending on the last peg in the row.

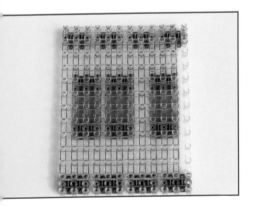

6. Repeat this pattern all the way up the rest of the loom, looping up from your last row, then looping across the pegs where you ended your loops, moving out from the center peg in the row. When you reach the second to last row on the loom, stop after you loop your row moving out from the center, and don't loop bands up to the final row.

7. Start at the second peg in the top row, and connect it to the peg below it. Move to the next peg to the right and do the same. Continue across the top row of your rectangle, like you did along the bottom earlier.

8. Triple-loop a band, and then slide it onto the middle peg in the top row.

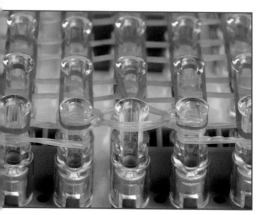

9. Rotate the loom so the arrows are pointed away from you.

10. On the middle peg where you put your triple-looped band, hook the second band and lift it up and off, looping it back onto the peg where the other end is hooked. Repeat this for the next band on the peg and again for the last one.

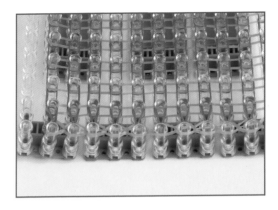

11. Move to the next peg to the left and repeat the process, starting with the second rubber band and looping each band back onto the peg where it started. Do the same with all of the pegs in the row, finishing the pegs on the left, then repeating the process with the pegs to the right of the center peg.

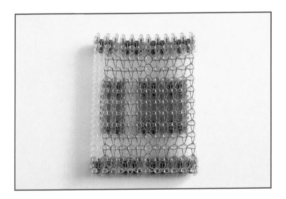

12. Starting at the middle peg in the next row up, repeat the unlooping process, hooking the second band on the peg and looping it back onto the peg where it began. Continue to loop the rest of the rows inside your rectangle in the same way, moving up the loom row by row and working your way from the middle peg, first to the left, then to the right. Do not do the last row yet.

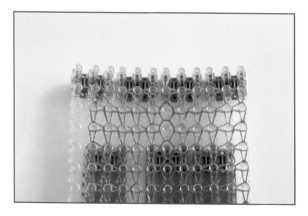

13. On the last row, start at the peg at the top left corner of your rectangle. Hook the second rubber band on the peg and pull it up and off the peg, looping it onto the peg to the right. Continue looping like this until you get to the middle peg, and then do the same starting at the corner peg on the right.

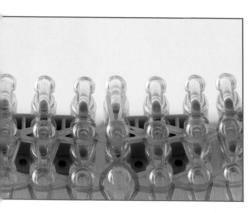

14. When you reach the middle peg, grab the bottom rubber band with your hook and pull it up and off the peg and back to the peg above it.

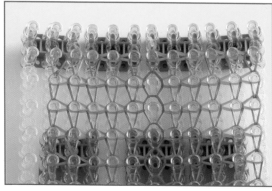

15. Secure the loops on this last peg with a c-clip.

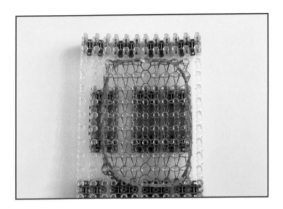

16. Remove your project from the loom, starting with the tightest edge, and then pull the rest off the loom.

Now just stretch the case over the back of your phone, and you are good to go! If the case is too big, you can try again with three looms instead of four; just be sure you always have an odd number of columns or the case will come unraveled.

CANDY CANE ORNAMENT

Create a festive candy cane ornament to celebrate the holiday season! This simple project is decorative and fun, but it definitely will not taste like peppermint stick, so try not to eat it when you are done!

You need:

2 looms • hook • c-clip
36 RED and 33 WHITE rubber bands

1. Set up your looms beside each other with the arrows pointing away from you. Flip the two columns on the right so the arrows are pointing toward you. Loop a white band around the peg at the bottom left corner, and connect it to the peg to the right. Loop another white band around the corner peg, and connect it to the next peg above it.

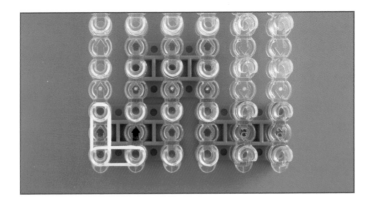

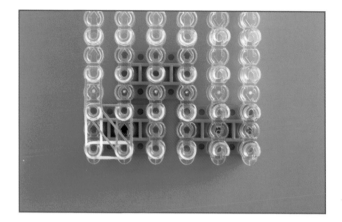

2. Loop a red band around the second peg in the bottom row, and connect it to the peg above it. Loop a red band around that peg, and connect it to the peg to the left. Loop another red band around the second peg in the first row, and connect it up and to the left. Loop another red band around the second peg in the first column, and connect it to the peg above it.

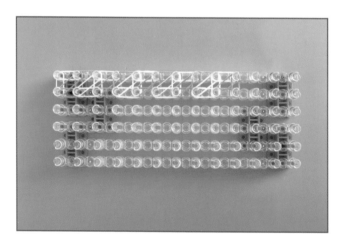

3. Starting on the second peg in the second row, repeat step 2, using white bands. Continue to repeat step 2 in this way, alternating red and white bands, with your last band ending on the third peg from the end of the loom.

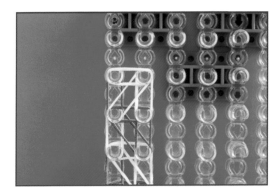

4. Loop a white band over the fourth peg from the end in the second column, and connect it to the peg above it. Loop another white band over the fourth band from the end in the first column, and connect it to the peg up and to the right. Loop one white band over the third peg from the end in the first column, and connect it to the peg to the right.

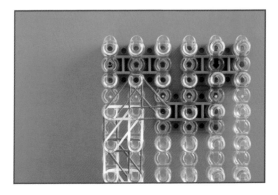

5. Loop a red band around the third peg from the top in the first column, and connect it to the peg up and to the right. Loop a red band around the third peg from the end in the second column, and connect it to the peg above; then loop another band around the same peg, and connect it to the peg to the right. Loop a red band around the peg where you just ended your loop, and connect it to the peg up and to the left.

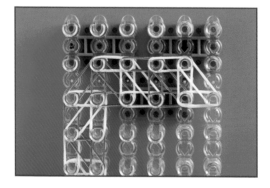

6. Loop a white band around the peg at the top of your last red triangle, and connect it to the peg to the right. Loop a white band around the peg where you ended your loop, and connect it to the next peg down. From that peg, loop another white band to the next peg on the right, then loop a white band around that peg and connect it to the peg up and to the left, where you started your triangle. Repeat twice more, alternating colors.

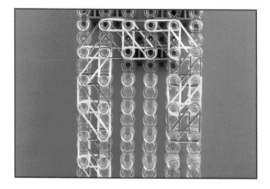

7. Loop a red band around the third peg down in the second to last row, and connect it to the peg below. Do the same with the third peg in the last column. Loop a red band around the fourth peg from the end in the second to last column, and connect it to the peg up and to the right. Loop another band on the same peg, and connect it to the right. Repeat this pattern twice more, starting at the next row down and alternating colors. Double-loop your last red band.

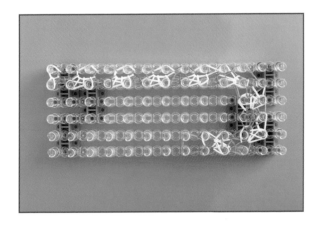

8. Start at the pegs you just double-looped. Hook the second band on the peg and loop it back to the peg where it started. Loop the rest of the project in this way, working your way back to the beginning of the candy cane.

9. After you remove the candy cane from the looms, you can fit a hook into the top of the cane to make decorating simple!

PEACE SIGN

Peace, love, and magic looms! This far-out peace sign comes together quickly and looks cool hanging in your window or on your wall!

1. Set up the loom with the middle column set one peg closer to you and with the arrow pointing away from you. Loop a band around the first middle peg, and connect it to the next peg above it. Repeat until you reach the end of the loom.

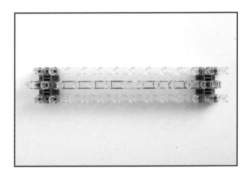

2. Loop a band around the first peg on the left, and connect it to the next peg above it. Repeat for five total bands. Do the same on the right side.

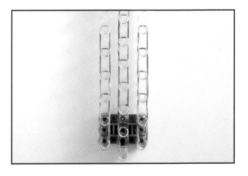

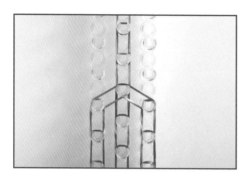

3. Loop a band around the sixth peg on the left side, and connect it to the peg up one and to the right. Loop a band around the sixth peg on the right, and connect it to the same middle peg.

4. Turn the loom around and, starting with the peg closest to you, pull the second band on each peg up and off, looping it back onto the peg where the other end is looped. Continue until you reach the end of the loom.

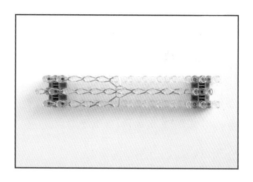

5. Pull your bands from the loom, and stretch them over your craft hoop.

6. Turn your loom so the arrow is pointing away from you. Loop a band around the first middle peg, and connect it to the peg up and to the left. Loop a band around the peg you ended on and connect it up and to the right. Continue this zigzag pattern until you reach the end of the loom.

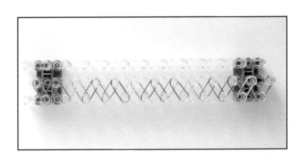

7. Lay your craft hoop over your zigzag pattern. Starting at the second looped peg on the end, hook the second band on the peg and pull it up and off, looping it over the craft hoop and back onto the peg

where the other end of the band is looped. Continue looping in this way all the way down the loom. As the bands are looped, pull them from the loom. Use a c-clip to secure the final band, or leave your hook on the loop to keep it from unraveling. Lay out your zigzag pattern again. Remove the c-clip from the band on the craft hoop and slide both ends of the band onto the top middle peg of your zigzag. Starting on this peg, loop the bands on your loom over the craft hoop and back onto their starting pegs as you did before.

8. Repeat steps 6 and 7 until you have covered your craft hoop.
   Secure the final loop with a c-clip, then connect it to the
   starting loop on the loom.

BLOOMING BEADED BRACELET

Take the Daisy Chain Bracelet and jazz it up! This neat bouquet of a bracelet adds cool beads to the "flowers," making it extra special and beautiful! Whether you like pretty pinks and blues or prefer the colors of your favorite sports team and beads that look like soccer balls or footballs, mix and match to make it your own!

You need:

1 loom • hook • c-clip • 15 beads
67 rubber bands

1. Set up your loom with the middle pegs pulled one closer to you and the arrow pointing away from you. Loop a band around the first middle peg, and connect it to the peg above it. Starting at the second middle peg, loop your bands to the left to make the first half of a hexagon, finishing on the fourth middle peg. Start again on the second middle peg, and loop your bands to the right in the same way to finish off your hexagon.

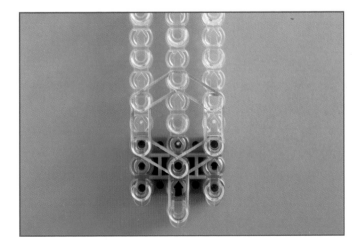

2. To make your "petals," loop a band around the third middle peg (in the center of your hexagon), and connect it to the peg up and to the right. Thread the *second* rubber band "petal" through a bead, then loop another band around the middle peg, and connect it to the peg down and to the right. Continue to connect all six of the outer pegs in this way, moving clockwise around the hexagon and switching off with a bead every other band.

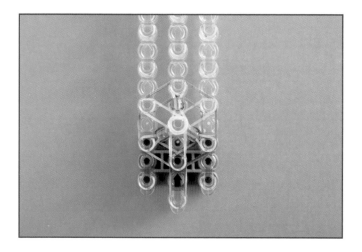

3. Triple-loop a band and put it on the middle peg of your hexagon.

4. Starting on the last middle peg of your hexagon, repeat your pattern: loop both sides of a new hexagon, then add the bands from the center. With the second "flower," add the bead on the *first* "petal," and then trade off beading every other petal. Finish with a triple-looped cap band on the middle peg. Repeat this up the loom until you have five hexagons total, trading off between placing the beads on the first and second "petals." On the final hexagon, before you lay down your bands, loop a band

around the last middle peg in the pattern and connect it to the last peg in the middle row, then complete the final flower pattern.

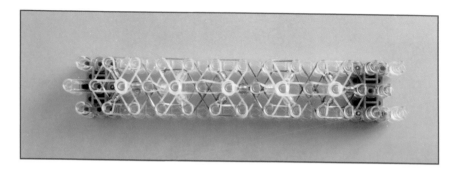

5. Turn the loom around so the arrow is facing toward you. Start looping the bands of your "petals" back onto the pegs where they started: First, loop the bands from the center of the hexagon, starting with the first band under the cap band, then loop counterclockwise around your hexagon. Next, loop the bands that make up the hexagon, starting from the left half and then the right in the same way you placed the bands in the very first step. Loop all of the "flowers" this way, making your way to the end of the loom.

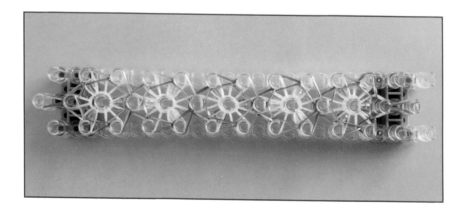

6. Loop the last band back to the remaining peg. Attach a c-clip to secure the last band, and then remove your project from the loom.

7. For added length, loop more rubber bands through the end bands before attaching the c-clip.

SPORTS FAN
KEY CHAIN

Show your team pride or school spirit with this customizable key chain! The stretchy loop slips over your wrist so you'll never lose your keys, even while you cheer your team on!

You need:

2 looms • hook • key clip • c-clip several beads • 27 bands for the loop • 38 bands for the keychain

1. Set up your looms end to end with the pegs square and the arrow pointing away from you. Remove the center pegs. Loop a band over the bottom left peg, and connect it to the third peg up.

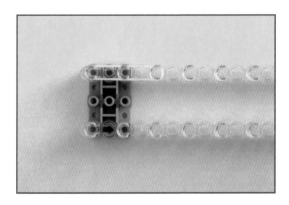

2. Move to the second peg in the column, and connect it to the third peg above it. Repeat all the way up the loom. Do the same on the right side.

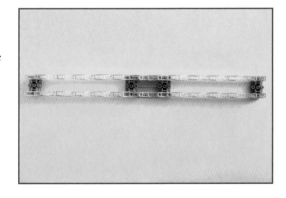

3a. Loop a band around the second peg from the end in the left column. Connect it to the peg above it. Do the same on the right side.

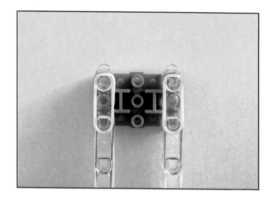

3b. Double-loop a band and connect it to both end pegs.

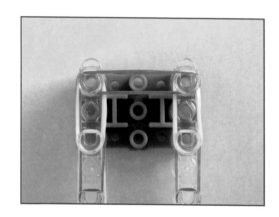

4. Turn your loom so the arrow points toward you. Starting with the pegs closest to you, hook the second band on the peg and pull it up and off, looping it back to the peg where it started.

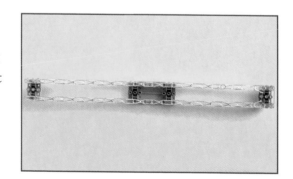

5. Secure the end loops with a c-clip or your hook for now. Pull the project off the loom.

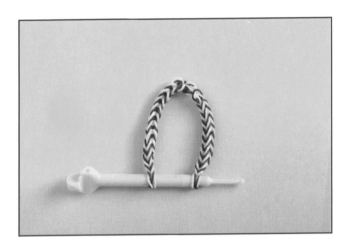

6. Set up a single loom with the pegs offset, with middle pegs closer to you and with the arrow pointing away from you. Starting on the first middle peg, loop a band around the peg, and connect it to the next peg up and to the left. Loop a band around that peg, and connect it to the next peg up in the row. Continue looping this way to the end of the loom, ending your last loop on the last middle peg. Start again at the first middle peg, and do the same for the right side.

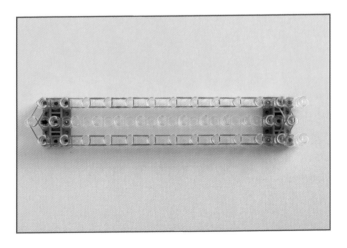

7. Loop a band around the first peg on the left, and connect it to the first peg on the right. Repeat until you reach the end of the loom. To add beads, thread the band through the bead before putting it on the loom. Letter beads should go in the order shown, with the words starting at the opposite end from where you started laying out the project.

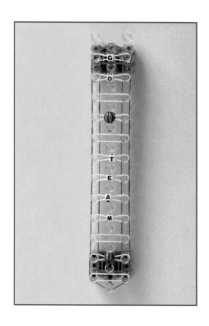

8. Attach the first half of your project to your loom, sliding all of the loops onto the peg above your first letter bead.

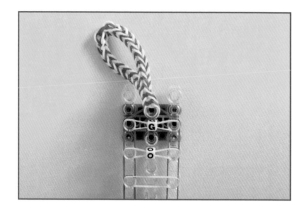

9. Starting with that same top middle peg, hook the band below the bands you just added, and pull it off the peg, looping it back onto the peg where it started. Loop both bands off this first middle peg, then loop the rest of the project the same way, working towards the other end of the loom.

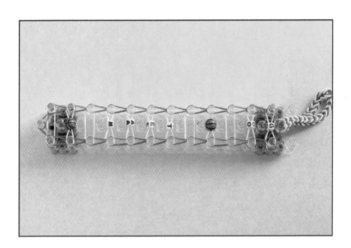

10. Secure the final loops with a c-clip and attach a key clip.

RAiNBOW RiNG

Show off your rubber band skills with this impressive piece of bling! Use brightly colored beads to make this ring really pop, or make like the big leagues and use sports beads for a championship ring!

1. Set up your loom with the middle pegs closer to you and the arrow pointing away. Loop a band around the peg closest to you, and then connect it to the peg above it. Loop a band around the second middle peg, and connect it to the peg up and to the right. Loop another band around the second middle peg, and connect it up and to the left. Loop two bands up on either side of the loom. Loop a band around the fifth peg in the middle column, and connect it to the peg above it. Then loop a band around the fourth peg in the right column, and connect it to the peg where you ended your last loop. Do the same on the left.

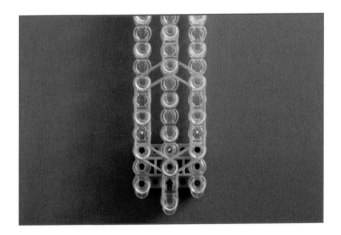

2. To add your beads, thread
a band through a bead
and loop one end around
the first middle peg in
your hexagon. Connect
the other end of the band
up and to the right, then
repeat with the rest of the
pegs as shown, moving
clockwise until you have
looped five beaded bands.

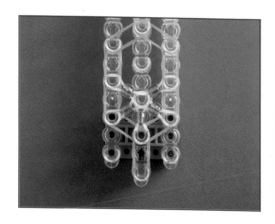

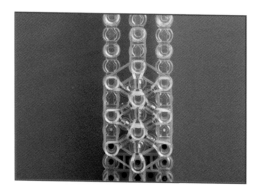

3. Repeat step 2 on the
next middle peg in your
hexagon. Loop your first
beaded band to the peg
up and to the right, then
loop the rest of the pegs
around the middle peg,
moving clockwise. This
time you will connect a
band to the middle peg
below.

4. Triple-loop a cap band
onto both middle pegs
in the hexagon.

5. Turn your loom so the arrow points toward you. Start with the triple-looped peg closest to you. Hook the first band under the cap band and pull it off, looping it back to the peg where it started, which should

be the peg directly beneath the middle peg. Continue looping around the circle this way, moving counterclockwise, until you have looped all the bands off the peg. Do the same with the next middle peg, looping the first band under the cap band off and back to where the other end of the band is looped, which should be the peg to the bottom right of the center peg. Continue looping the bands off the middle peg in this way, moving counterclockwise. When you have finished all the bands on the two middle pegs, loop the outside bands, starting with the three bands on the second middle peg closest to you and then working up both sides. Finish by looping the top middle peg.

6. Secure both loose ends with a c-clip. Fasten the two ends together to make your ring! If it is too tight, loop a few bands together and connect them to the c-clip to make it bigger.

PENCIL TOPPER

Make writing and drawing even more fun by giving your pencils some extra flare! This pencil topper is super easy to make and can fit over your pencils and pens or can be made into a key ring for even more loom entertainment!

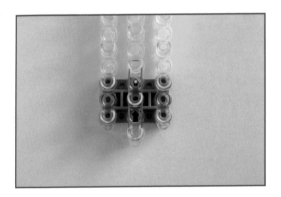

1. Start with the loom offset with the center pegs closer to you and the arrow pointing away. Loop a band over the first middle peg, and connect it to the third peg up.

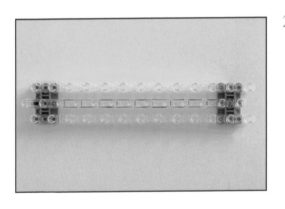

2. Loop a band around the next peg up, and connect it to the third peg above it. Continue looping the middle pegs this way all the way up the loom, until there is one empty peg left at the top of the loom.

3. Loop a band over the middle peg where you ended your last band, and connect it to the peg below it.

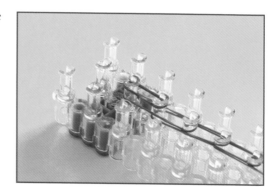

4. Loop a band around the second to last peg in the middle column, and connect it to the peg up and to the left. Loop another band around the second middle peg, and connect it to the next peg up. Loop another band around the second middle peg, and connect it to the next peg up and to the right.

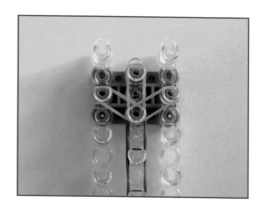

5. Repeat step 4 until you cannot fit any more bands on the peg. This example uses twenty-four total bands, eight for each peg.

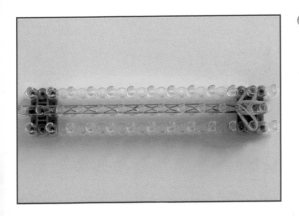

6. Starting at the second middle peg from the end (where you stacked all of the bands for the charm), loop the bottom band (the green band here) and pull it off the peg, looping it back onto the peg where it started. Continue looping this way as you work your way down the loom back to where you started.

7. Slide your pencil through the bands on the second peg, and then remove your project from the loom!

NUNCHUKS

Rubber bands meet martial arts! Nunchuks are an awesome tool used in karate and Okinawan kobudō, which are forms of Japanese martial arts. They help improve speed and hand movements in training, but they look really cool, too! These nunchuks are made mostly of rubber bands, but be careful— there is metal wire to keep them firm, so never use these in a way that might hurt someone. Try out this great project and have fun!

You need:

1 loom • hook • 2 c-clips
2 metal craft wires • 143 bands

1. Set up your loom with the pegs square and the arrow pointing away from you. Loop a band around the first center peg, and connect it to the peg to the left. Loop another band on the center peg, and connect it to the peg to the right. Loop a band around each peg in the first row, and connect the peg to the next one above it. Loop a band around the left peg in the first row, and connect it to the next middle peg. Do the same with the right peg in the first row.

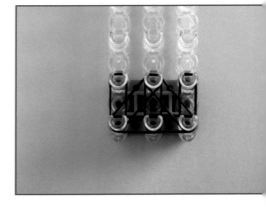

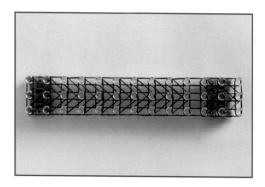

2. Repeat your pattern on each row of the loom until you reach the end.

3. Triple-loop a band over the center peg in the top row of the loom.

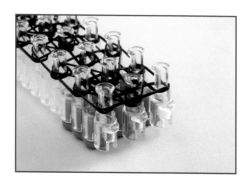

4. Lay your craft wire over your loom bent double, as shown, with the bent end resting above the top middle peg. Starting with the second band on the top middle peg, loop the bands up and off the peg and over the craft wire, hooking them back onto the peg

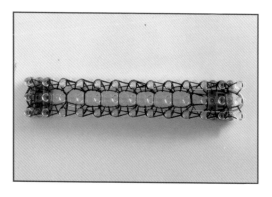

where the other end of the band is looped. After the center peg, loop the side pegs in the same way, then move to the next row and repeat. On the final row, loop the bands from the corner pegs onto the center peg.

5. Secure the loose bands with the c-clips, and remove your project from the loom. Repeat the steps to make a second nunchuk.

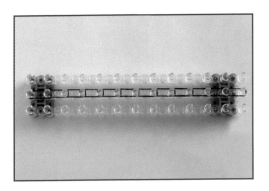

6. Loop a line of bands down the center of your loom. Turn the loom around, and loop the bands back onto the pegs where they started.

7. Remove the chain from the loom and attach either end to the c-clips of the nunchuks.

TRiPLe-OCTO
SHOeLACe
CHARMS

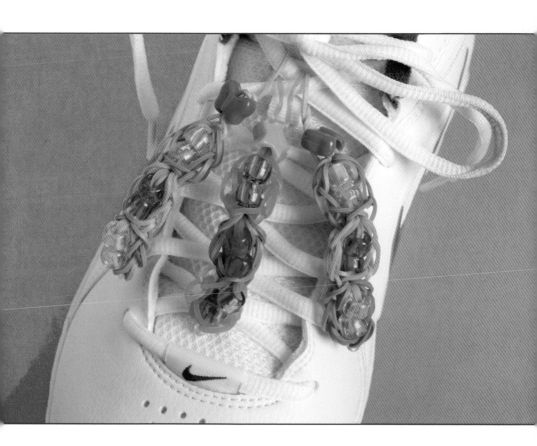

Make your kicks twice as cool with these Triple-Octo Shoelace Charms! You can customize them with different beads and colors to suit your style.

1. Set up your loom with the center pegs closer to you and the arrow pointing away from you. Starting on the center peg closest to you, do one Octo stitch: loop three bands around to make the left side of the hexagon, then start at the first center peg and do the same on the right side. Thread a band through a bead, and attach it to the first and second middle peg. Thread another band through a bead and attach it to the second and third middle pegs.

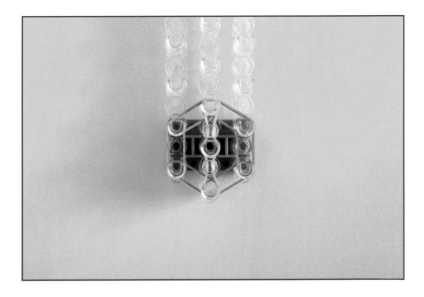

2. Starting on the middle peg where you ended your last Octo, do two more Octo stitches in the same way. Thread a band through a bead, attach the band to the top middle peg in your last Octo, and then connect it to the next peg above it. Loop a band around that peg, and connect it to the peg above it.

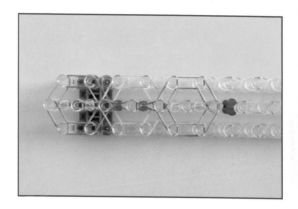

3. Turn the loom so the arrow points toward you. Starting with the looped pegs closest to you, loop the bands off the pegs and back onto the pegs where they began. Always hook the second unlooped band on the peg and loop it, looping all of the bands on a peg before moving on to the next peg. Loop all of the pegs in this way, working your way to the end of the loom.

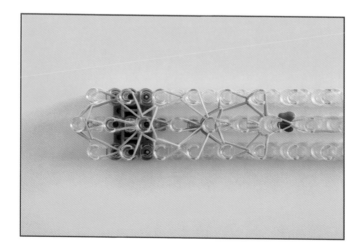

4. Secure the loose bands on the final peg with a c-clip or tie it off with another rubber band. Remove your charm from the loom.

5. Make two more Triple-Octo charms in the same way. Hook all the end loops together with a c-clip and attach to your shoelaces!

SPORTS BAND

Cheer on your team with this sports-themed band! Change up the beads and the colors to match your team's uniform—you can make a different one for all your favorite teams!

1. Set up your loom with the middle pegs closer to you and the arrow pointing away from you. Loop a band around the first center peg, and connect it to the peg up and to the left. Do the same on the other side. Starting with the pegs where you ended your bands, loop a line of bands up both outside columns on the loom, looping the last bands onto the last middle peg.

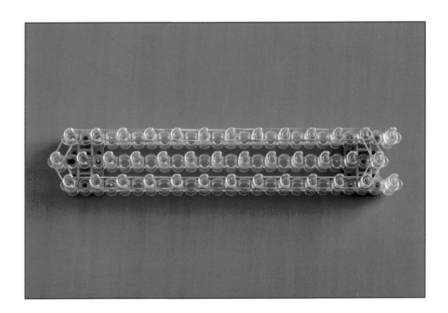

2. Thread a band through a sports bead, and loop it over the outside pegs in the second row. Continue up the loom in this way, stretching the beaded bands across the columns you created.

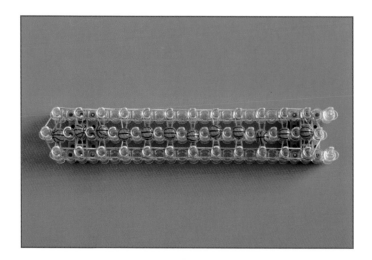

3. Triple-loop a band on the last middle peg.

4. Turn the loom so the arrow is pointing toward you. Hook the second band on the middle peg closest to you, and pull it off the peg, looping it back to the peg where it started. Loop all the bands off the closest middle peg this way, then loop the rest of the bands along the outside of the loom, working your way to the middle peg at the other end of the loom. Do not loop the beaded bands.

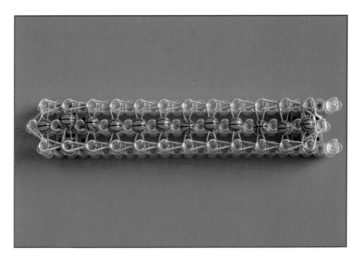

5. Secure the loops on the final peg with a rubber band or a c-clip. Remove your project from the loom.

PiNNACLe CHOKeR PENDANT

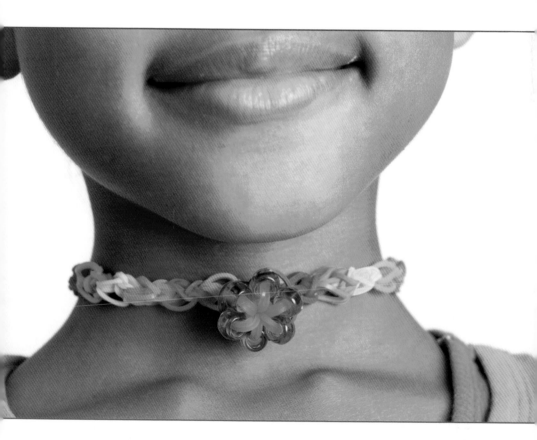

Jazz up your necklace by adding a gorgeous pendant! This extra step will take your jewelry from simple to sophisticated—choose your favorite color of the rainbow, or try using every color to continue the cool rainbow effect!

You need:
3 looms • hook • c-clip • 6 beads
15 rubber bands

To Make the Choker:

1. Set up three looms the long way, with the arrows pointing toward you. Lay out the pattern for the Pinnacle Bracelet (page 9), repeating until you reach the end of the third loom.

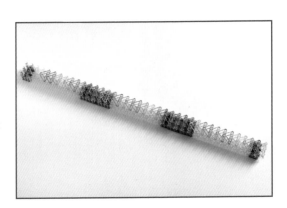

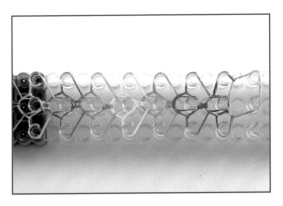

2. Loop the bands back to the pegs where they started, as usual, then secure the loose bands on the final peg with a c-clip.

Remove the choker from the loom and set aside.

To Make the Pendant:

1. Set up your loom
   with the middle
   pegs closer to you
   and the arrow
   pointing away
   from you. Loop a
   band around the
   first middle peg,
   and connect it
   to the peg above

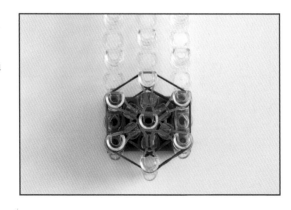

   it. Starting at the second middle peg, loop your bands to the
   left to make the first half of a hexagon, finishing on the fourth
   middle peg. Start again on the second middle peg, and loop
   your bands to the right in the same way to finish off your
   hexagon.

2. To make the spokes that will feature the beads, thread six
   bands with your six beads. With the first beaded band, loop it
   around the third middle peg (in the center of your hexagon),
   and connect it to the peg up and to the right. Continue to
   connect all six of the outer pegs with the beaded bands in

   this way, moving
   clockwise around
   the hexagon. Then,
   triple-loop a band
   on the middle peg
   of your hexagon as
   a cap band.

3. Triple-loop another band on the fourth middle peg (the top of your hexagon) as another cap band. Turn the loom around so the arrow is facing toward you. Start looping the bands of your spokes 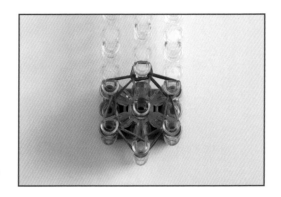 back onto the pegs where they started: First, loop the bands from the center of the hexagon, starting with the first band under the cap band, then loop counterclockwise around your hexagon. Next, loop the outer bands, starting from the left half and then the right in the same way you placed the bands in the very first step.

4. Loop the last band back to the remaining peg. Attach a c-clip to secure the last band, and then remove your project from the loom. Attach the pendant to the middle of the choker, or make several pendants and line the whole thing!

SNOWMAN ORNAMENT

It's getting frosty out there! Get into the winter spirit by using this cool snowman as an ornament or decoration, attaching it to your backpack, or gluing it to a refrigerator magnet. Luckily, he won't melt!

For the Snowman's Head:

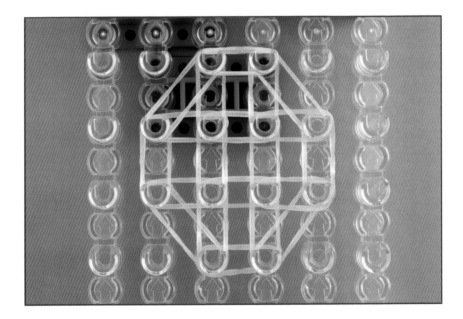

1. Connect two looms side by side with the arrow pointing away from you. Loop a band around the two middle pegs of the row. Loop bands around each of these pegs, and connect them to the pegs above them. Loop a band around the left middle peg, and connect it to the peg up and to the left. Loop a band around the right middle peg, and connect it to the peg up and to the right.

2. Loop a row of bands across the four pegs in the next row where you ended your last loops. Loop bands around each of these four pegs, and connect them to the peg above them.

3. Loop across the pegs where you ended your last loops again, moving from left to right. Connect the two middle bands in this row to the pegs above them.

4. Connect the outside pegs in this row up and diagonally toward the middle of the loom as shown. Double-loop a cap band around the top two pegs in the shape.

5. Starting at the top two pegs of the circle, loop the bands back onto the pegs where they started, first looping the second band on the peg, then working your way down the peg.

6. Hook your pattern in the opposite way you put it on the loom, hooking the loops down, then from right to left.

7. Secure the loose bands with a c-clip.

8. Remove your circle from the loom and put aside.

For the Snowman's Torso:

You need:

2 looms • hook • c-clip • 41 bands

1. Set up your looms side by side with the arrow pointing away from you, and repeat the pattern you did for the head circle, laying out the shape as shown. This will require more bands to make a larger circle.

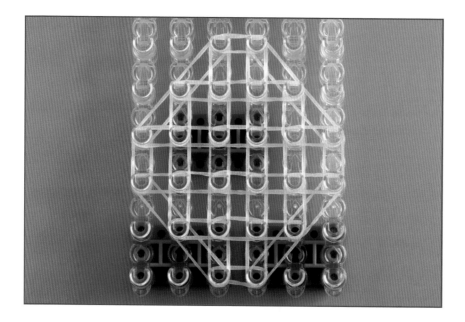

2. Loop bands from right to left, then loop up to the next row, using diagonal loops to make your circle wider in the center, then smaller at the end.

3. Finish your pattern with a double-loop cap band across the top middle pegs. Hook your bands back onto the pegs where they started, beginning with the top middle pegs. Always hook the second unlooped band on the peg.

4. Loop all of the bands on a peg before moving to the next peg: loop down from the top row, then across from right to left, then repeat.

5. Secure the loose bands on the final pegs with a c-clip.

6. Remove your circle from the loom and set it aside.

For the Snowman's Base:

1. Set up your looms with two connected side by side, adding two additional columns.

2. Create your circle as you did with the smaller circles, laying the shape out as shown. Don't forget to secure the pattern with a double-loop cap band across the top middle pegs.

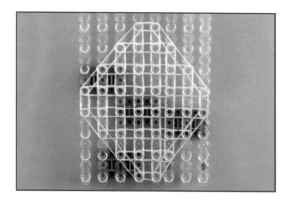

3. Hook the bands back as you did before.

4. Secure the loose bands on the final pegs and remove your circle from the loom.

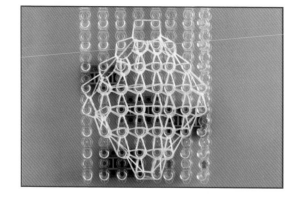

To Assemble Your Snowman:

1. Connect your three circles with the c-clips, as shown.

2. Double-loop a band around the head and body circles to make a scarf.

3. Knot two brown bands together, loop the end through the body circle, and pull the other end of the band through the loop to secure it. Do the same for the other arm.

4. Add the face and buttons by pulling bands through the project from the back, leaving the loose ends in the back.

ROCKER CUFF BRACELET

Rock and roll with this awesome, stylish cuff bracelet! Make a cuff with all one color, or make a whole rainbow to go up your arm!

You need:

4 looms • hook • 5 c-clips • 100 DARK GREEN bands • 100 LIGHT GREEN bands • 100 LIME GREEN bands • 76 WHITE bands (plus 1 extra band of each color to connect the cuffs)

1. Set up your four looms side by side, with the arrows pointing right. Starting at the bottom left-hand corner, loop dark green bands across the bottom row of the loom, looping from left to right. Loop a dark green band around the peg in the bottom left corner, and then attach it to the next peg above. Do the same with the rest of the pegs in the first row. Loop across the second row with the dark green bands again, going from left to right.

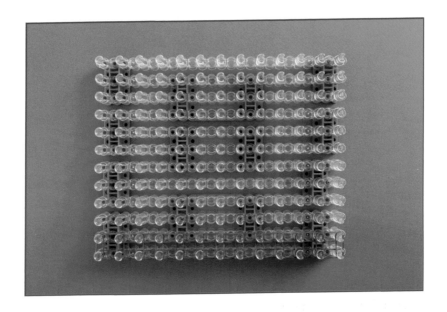

2. Loop another set of dark green bands coming up from this row as you did before. Then loop across the third row in your next color (light green), looping left to right. Repeat this process all the way up the

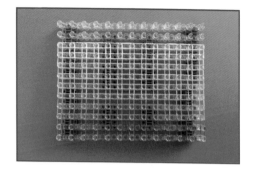

loom, looping across a row, up, across, and up once more before switching to the next color. For the white bands, repeat the same process, but you will not need a final row of vertical loops.

3. Triple-loop a cap band and put it onto the peg on the top right (which will be a white band).

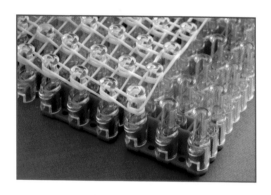

4. Starting with the peg with the cap band, begin looping your project by hooking the band right below the cap band, pulling it up and off the peg, and looping it back onto the peg where it started. First loop the top row from right to left, and then loop the vertical bands. Repeat this process for each row.

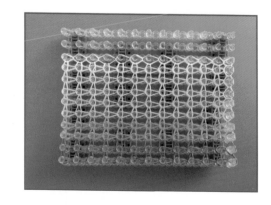

5. Attach a c-clip to the band on the lower left. Remove the first half of your cuff from the loom.

6. Repeat these steps for the second half of your cuff. Once you have both sides of your cuff, attach them together by looping a band through the end of the cuff with the corresponding end of the other side. Do this with five bands, one for each color in the cuff. Attach these bands to c-clips to secure. Now you have a great, stylish cuff!

BLiNG RiNG

Don't settle for a plain ring; go big and make a bling ring! This beautiful piece of jewelry combines a ring and a bracelet—it's fit for a fashionista!

To Make the Stone:

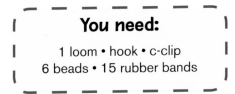

You need:

1 loom • hook • c-clip
6 beads • 15 rubber bands

1. Set up your loom with the middle pegs pulled closer to you and the arrow pointing away from you. Loop a band around the first middle peg, and connect it to the peg above it. Loop a band around the fourth middle peg, and connect it to the peg above it. Starting at the second middle peg, loop your bands to the left to make the first half of a hexagon, finishing on the fourth middle peg. Start again on the second middle peg, and loop your bands to the right in the same way to finish off your hexagon.

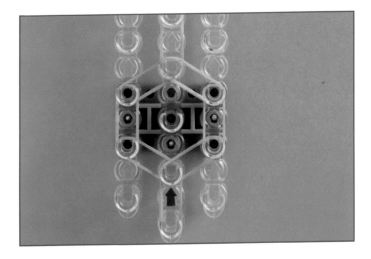

2. To make the spokes that will feature the beads, thread six bands with your six beads. With the first beaded band, loop it around the third middle peg (in the center of your hexagon), and connect it to the peg up and to the right. Continue to connect all six of the outer pegs with the beaded bands in this

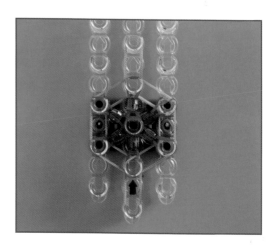

way, moving clockwise around the hexagon. Triple-loop a band on the middle peg of your hexagon as a cap band. Triple-loop another band on the fourth middle peg (the top of your hexagon) as another cap band.

3. Turn the loom around so the arrow is facing toward you. Start looping the bands of your spokes back onto the pegs where they started: First, loop the bands from the center of the hexagon, starting with the first band under the cap band, then loop counterclockwise around your hexagon. Next, loop the outer bands, starting from the left half and then the right in the same way that you placed the bands in the very first step.

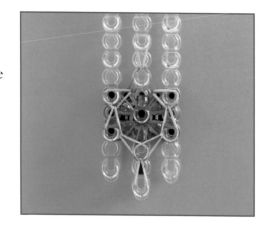

4. Loop the last band back to the last remaining peg. Attach a c-clip to secure the loose bands on either end, and then remove your project from the loom. Connect the c-clipped bands to make your ring band: loop several bands through one another to extend the band if it is too small.

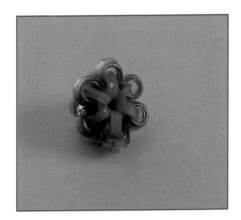

To Make the Bracelet:

You need:

1 loom • hook
c-clip • 50 bands

1. Lay your loom horizontally with the arrow pointing to your right. Move the middle row all the way down and attach it to the loom on the second-to-last peg, so that it looks like a big

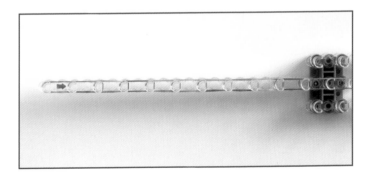

letter Y. Starting with the bottom of the Y, loop your first color from the first peg to the third peg (skipping the second peg). Loop your second color from the second peg to the fourth peg (skipping the third peg). Loop your third color from the third peg to the fifth peg (skipping the fourth peg). Repeat this pattern until you have reached the end of the row.

2. Now that you are at the base of the loom, loop a band from the second middle peg (the one that is next to last in the row) around the peg above it *and* the peg up and to the left of that peg (it will be the third peg in the first row). The loop will appear triangular. Loop another band from the same middle peg around the one above it and the one up and to the right (the third peg in the third row). The loop will appear triangular in the opposite direction. From the last peg in the middle row, loop a band around the peg up and to the left *and* the peg just above that one (the fourth peg in the first row). This loop will also appear triangular. From the last peg in the middle row, loop a band around the peg up and to the right *and* the peg just above that one as well (the fourth peg in the third row). This loop will appear triangular.

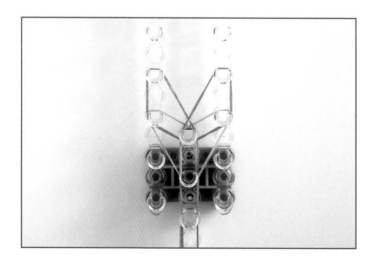

3. Like you did with the "tail," loop your bands down both outside rows,

starting from the third peg and stopping at the twenty-first peg, making sure that each band is looped across three pegs instead of two. Connect the last two pegs on both sides with a band to close the rectangle-shaped side on the loom.

4. Starting with the very end of the loom where you closed off the rectangle, work

backward and hook the bands back onto the pegs where they started. This means that each band will skip a peg, just as it did when you first placed it down.

5. Secure the loose loops on the final peg with a c-clip. Carefully remove the project from the loom. Attach the end with the c-clip to the underside of the stone to complete your bling ring!

ICE CREAM CONE

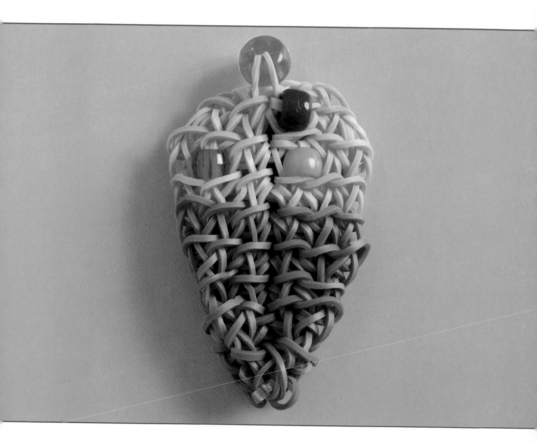

We all scream for ice cream! This super cool project looks so good it's delicious! Hang it from a string or a key chain, or pull it out when you want your favorite frozen treat!

> ## You need:
>
> 2 looms plus 1 row of pegs • hook
> c-clip • 98 rubber bands

1. Set up two looms side by side plus one extra row. To lay out the cone shape, loop a band around the first middle peg, and connect it up and to the left. Loop another band to the middle peg, and connect it up to the next peg above. Loop a third band around the middle peg, and connect it up and to the right. Loop two bands across in the second row to connect the pegs where you ended the bands from the first middle peg. Loop bands around each of the three pegs you connected, and then connect them to the pegs above. Loop from left to right across the pegs where you ended your last loops. Repeat this pattern up the loom, looping bands up then across from left to right, making the cone wider every other row as shown, by adding diagonal bands when you are looping up to the next row. Continue until your cone is as wide as you want it.

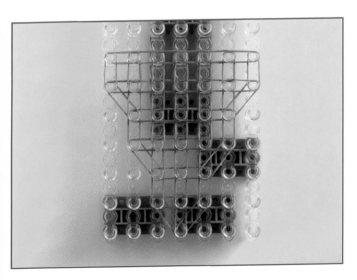

2. From your last row of cone bands, loop ice cream-colored bands around each peg in the row, and connect them to the pegs above them. Loop a row of ice cream bands from left to right across the pegs where you ended your last loops. Loop two total rows of the ice cream color, following the same looping pattern that you used for the cone. Then decrease the pattern to five pegs, and then three, as shown. Triple-loop a cap band, and put it on the top middle peg of your ice cream. As you add ice cream–colored bands, thread beads onto a few random bands before you put them on the loom.

3. Begin looping your pattern, starting with the top middle triple-looped peg. Hook the band below the triple-looped cap band, and loop it back onto the peg where it began. Loop all the bands on the peg this way, then loop the rest of the row the

same way, always starting with the second band on the peg. Loop row-by-row, starting at the middle peg and working your way out before moving to the next row.

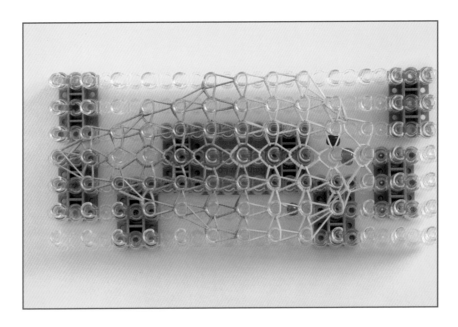

4. Secure the final loose loops with another rubber band or a c-clip. Remove your project from the loom.

LOOM
Magic Creatures!

PARROT

This feathered friend is cute and colorful! He's not too tricky; just pay attention to the color changes!

Difficulty level: **Medium**

You need:

1 loom • 1 hook • red, blue, yellow, black, and white bands

To Make the Legs:

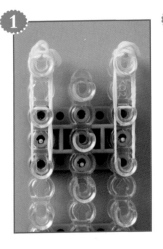 

1. Lay out your parrot's legs using single bands that have been wrapped once over themselves so they are tight. You can do this by wrapping a band twice around your hook and stretching it over the pegs. To make the feet, wrap a single yellow band around your hook four times and slide it onto a single yellow band that has been wrapped like the leg bands. Repeat three times for each foot.

2. Turn your loom and loop your legs. Secure the ends with a red band and put aside.

To Make the Tail:

 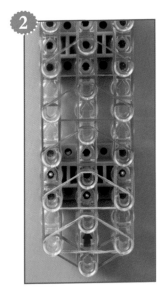

1. Attach double red bands to the first center pegs, and connect them to the right. Repeat and connect them to the left; then repeat one more time and connect to the center. Lay a line of double bands down each column, switching to blue as shown. You will have

a total of two red double bands and three blue double bands lining the outer columns and four red double bands and four blue double bands lining the center column. Wrap a blue cap band around each of the last pegs twice.

2. Wrap a red band around your hook twice and attach it to the first row in a triangle shape. Repeat four more times down the loom.

3. Turn your loom and loop your bands back to where they started. Secure the final loops with double red bands.

To Make the Wings:

1. Attach a single red band to the first middle peg, and connect it to the right. Lay a line of single bands down the middle and right columns, changing color, as shown. Wrap a red "holding" band around the fourth middle peg three times.

2. Wrap a yellow band around your hook twice, then attach it to the second pegs in the right and center columns. Repeat on the next two rows using blue bands. Wrap a blue cap band around the last peg in each row three times.

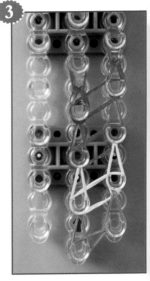

3. Turn your loom and loop your wing. Secure the loose loops and set it aside. Repeat to make your second wing.

To Make the Whole Body:

1. Using red double bands, lay out a hexagon shape onto the loom. Lay down the left side, then the right. Lay out a line of red double bands down the center of the hexagon.

2. Lay a larger hexagon shape onto your loom below the first, using red double bands. For the diagonal bands at the end, take the feet you set aside and untie the double red bands. Place the double bands at the bottom of the hexagon shape. Lay a line of red double bands down the center of the larger hexagon.

3. Place double red bands onto the second and third rows of the larger hexagon in a triangle shape. Take your wings and attach the loose loops to the first outside pegs in the larger hexagon shape, then attach the red "holding" band to the peg just above the feet.

4. To make the eyes, 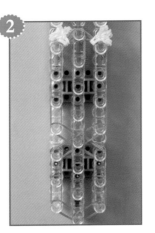 wrap a white band around your hook twice, then wrap a black band around your hook three times. Loop the first white band

around your hook two more times. Repeat to make your second eye. Thread the white and black bands onto a single red band.

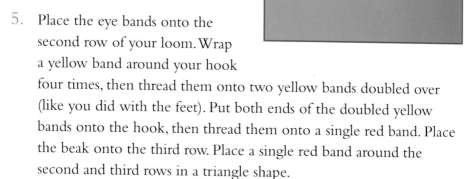

5. Place the eye bands onto the second row of your loom. Wrap a yellow band around your hook four times, then thread them onto two yellow bands doubled over (like you did with the feet). Put both ends of the doubled yellow bands onto the hook, then thread them onto a single red band. Place the beak onto the third row. Place a single red band around the second and third rows in a triangle shape.

6. Place the tail on the last peg on the loom.

7. Turn your loom and loop as usual. Secure the final loose loops with red double bands pulled in a slipknot.

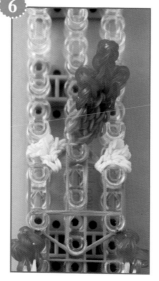

8. Remove your parrot!

BABY MOUSE

Say cheese! This little mouse makes a perfect pet because he doesn't bite or make a mess. Just don't let your cat catch him!

Difficulty level: **Easy**

You need:

1 loom • 1 hook • white, pink, and black bands

Set up your loom offset, with the middle column pulled one toward you and the arrow facing away.

1. Lay a line of pink bands all the way down your loom. Wrap the bands around the pegs twice; this keeps the bands tight. Wrap a pink cap band around the last peg four times. This is your mouse's tail.

2. Turn your loom and loop your bands back to where they started.

3. Remove your tail from the loom and set it aside.

4. Attach white double bands to the first middle peg, and connect them to the next middle peg. Attach white double bands to the second middle peg, connect them to the right, and then repeat and connect them to the left. Lay a line of double bands from the second middle peg to the fourth.

5. Lay out white double bands to finish your hexagon shape. Lay out the left side, then the right side.

6. Wrap a white band around your hook twice, then place it into the third row in a triangle shape.

7. Turn your loom around and loop your mouse's ear shape. Remove from the loom and repeat to make a second ear.

8. Attach a double white band to the first middle peg, and connect it to the next middle peg. Begin

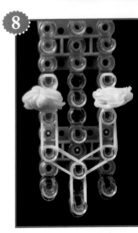
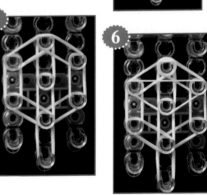
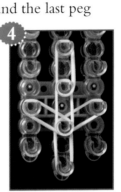

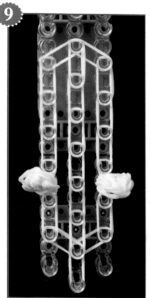

laying out a long hexagon shape: lay out the left side, then the right side. Use your hook to thread white double bands through the end loops of your ear shape and attach the bands to the third and fourth pegs in the outside columns.

9. Use double white bands to finish laying out your long hexagon shape. Lay a line of double white bands down the center of your shape.

10. Place the mouse's tail on the last center peg.

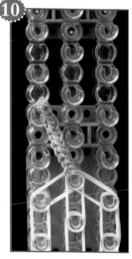

11. Wrap a white band around your hook twice, then place it on the third row in a triangle shape. Wrap two single black bands around your hook three times, then use your hook to thread them onto the triangle band you just placed on the loom.

12. Wrap a white band around your hook twice and place it onto the fourth row on the loom in a triangle shape. Repeat for rows 5 through 7.

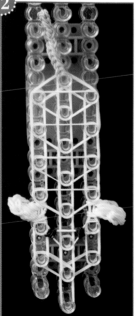

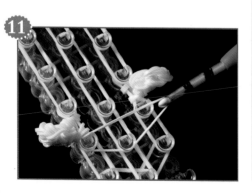

13. Turn your loom around and begin looping your bands back to where they started. When you reach the bands on the ear pegs, pull the ears through the loops before you loop them back onto the peg so that the ears remain standing.

14. Remove your mouse from the loom and thread a double pink band through the last white loops at his nose. Break a white band and use it to tie a knot around the pink bands between the nose and your hook. Cut the end of the pink bands and trim the white tie-off bands, then turn the pink bands so the knot is hidden in his snout.

DRAGON

This friendly dragon may not be a fire-breather, but he sure sets a spark. Although this project has several steps, it is well worth the effort! If you have some time and a couple of looms, you won't find a better pal than this cute little monster.

Difficulty level: **Medium**

You need:

2 looms • 1 hook • 2 black beads • dark green, lime green, and gold bands

Set up two looms connected side by side with  the middle column of both looms offset and pulled one peg closer to you.

1. Connect the first two middle pegs on your combined loom with double green bands. Attach two green bands to each of the middle pegs, and connect them to the next peg up and away from the center.

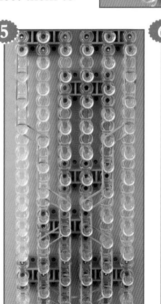

2. Attach two more green bands to each middle peg, and connect them to the next peg in the column.

3. Continue laying a line of double green bands up the two middle columns, ending on the fourth peg.

4. Using green double bands, lay out a circle shape for your dragon's head.

5. Using green double bands, lay out the body shape, as shown.

6. Lay double bands down both center columns; use lime green bands for his tummy.

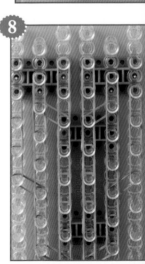

7. Lay out more double bands down the four middle columns to fill in his belly shape.

8. Lay lime green bands down the two center columns, starting where your last green bands left

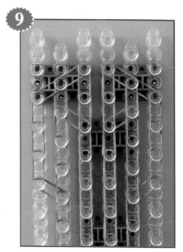

off (the tenth peg) and ending on the second-to-last peg.

9. Lay down a diagonal line of dark green double bands, starting at the outside column where you ended the dark green body bands and ending on the second-to-last middle peg. Do the same on both sides.

To Make the Feet:

1. Wrap three green bands onto your hook three times. Use your hook to "knit" a chain two loops long with the three wrapped bands on the end. (See Glossary for knitting instructions.)

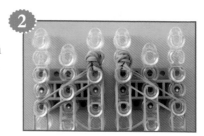

2. Place the four loose loops on your hook onto the second-to-last peg from the end in the middle column. Repeat to make the other foot.

To Make the Ears:

1. Wrap two bands around your hook three times. Use your hook to "knit" a chain one loop long with the two triple-looped bands on the end.

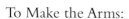

2. Place the loose loops from your hook onto the second peg in the column one in from the outside. Do the same on the other side for the other ear.

To Make the Arms:

1. Wrap two dark green bands onto your hook three times. Use your hook to "knit" a chain four loops long with the two wrapped bands at the end.

2. Slide all the loose loops from your arm onto the sixth peg, one column in. Repeat to make a second arm, and attach it on the other side.

To Make the Tail:

1. Wrap a dark green band around your hook three times. Use your hook to "knit" a chain eight loops long with the wrapped band at the end.

2. On your last stitch, leave the other end of the two bands off the hook. Stretch a single band between your hook and your finger.

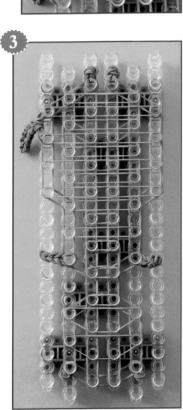

3. Thread the two bands from your hook onto the single band, then slide both ends of the single band onto the hook. Thread the remaining two loops from your tail onto a single band in the same way.

4. Attach your tail to the loom.

Looping Your Dragon:

1. Wrap a cap band twice around the two middle pegs in the fourth, fifth, sixth, and seventh rows.

2. Stretch a single band in a trapezoid shape, as shown, starting at the two middle pegs in the second row, and then repeat in the third row.

3. Lay vertical bands across your dragon's body shape.

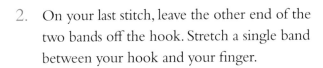

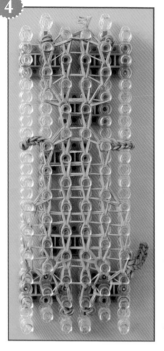

4. Starting at your dragon's feet, begin looping your bands back to where they started.

5. Secure the final loose loops on the loom. Remove your dragon.

To Make the Snout and Eyes:

1. Wrap three dark green bands onto your hook three times. Use your hook to "knit" a chain two loops long with the three bands at the end.

2. Remove your loops from the hook. Pull one end of the loops through the other end and pull it tight.

3. Use your hook to pull the single loop from the snout through the back of the dragon, then pull it through a different loop back to the front. Put the snout through the loop to secure it. Do the same for the other side.

4. Thread a single green band through a black bead. Use your hook to pull the loops from the single band to the back of the dragon's head, and secure them with a c-clip.

To Make the Wings:

1. Set up one loom offset, with the middle column pulled toward you one peg.

2. Attach two gold bands to the first middle peg, and connect them to the next peg to the right. Attach two more gold bands, and connect them to the left. Then attach two more gold bands to the center peg, and connect them to the next middle peg.

3. Lay a line of gold double bands down each column, ending on the fifth peg in the left and middle columns and the fourth peg in the right column.

4. Wrap a single gold band around the pegs in the second row twice to make a triangle shape. Continue laying triangle shapes down your wing shape, as shown.

5. Wrap a single cap band twice around each of the last pegs in your three columns.

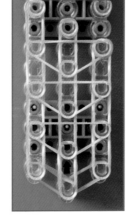

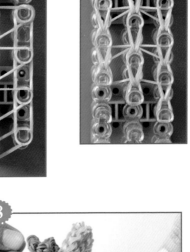

6. Turn your loom around. Loop all of the bands back to the first middle peg. Loop two green bands through the loops on the last peg, and pull it tight.

7. Remove your wing from the loom.

8. Stick your hook through the front of your dragon, and pull the two green bands from your wing though.

9. Put your hook through the back of the dragon and pull the bands back through another loop. Pull the wing through the bands to secure it.

10. Repeat to make and attach the other wing.

SANTA

Santa is coming to your loom! This jolly figure is great for Christmas or any time of year. Be prepared to show off your best loom skills, because this project takes a lot of time and concentration! You will need an extended loom, meaning two looms attached vertically. You will also need two extra columns on either side of the top loom for his big belly. We know this is a lot, so if you only have one loom, consider sharing looms with friends and working on this project as a team. Merry looming!

Difficulty level: **Hard**

You need:

2 looms + 2 columns • 1 regular hook • 1 fine hook • 1 c-clip • red, white, pink, and black bands • 1 gold band

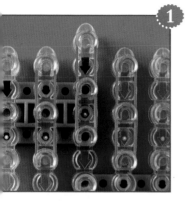

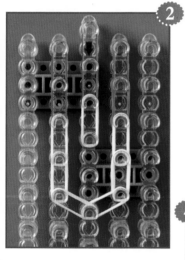

Set up a loom with the center column offset one peg away from you. All of the bands will be double bands except for the neck.

1. For each of the middle three columns, attach two rows of red double bands to make his hat, as shown.

2. To make his head, you will use white double bands for his white hair, laying them out, as shown.

3. Add two sets of double bands inside his face. We used pink bands for this Santa's face, but you can use whatever color you like.

4. Attach a white triple band for his neck. Just below, use red double bands for the shoulders and belly.

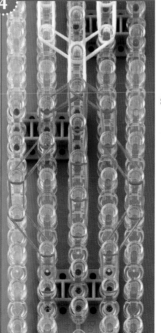

5. For Santa's legs, add three more sets of red double bands for both the second and

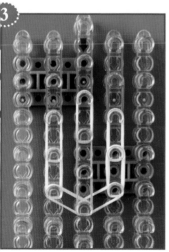

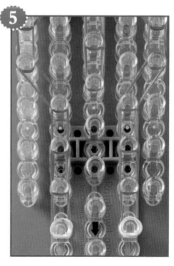

third columns. For the white fluffy cuff, triple-loop two single white bands and place each on the pegs in the second and third column.

6. Attach red double bands to the second and third columns, and then a set of black triple bands for each boot.

7. For the sole of his boot, take a black triple band and wrap it around your hook three times like a knot. Then take two bands and attach one end to the hook.

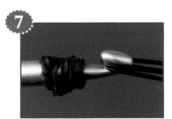

8. Slide the knot down the hook and over the bands.

9. Fold the bands and connect them to the pegs at the bottom of his legs for the boots.

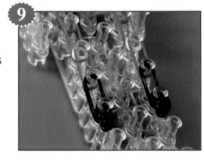

10. Fill in his belly with red double bands, as shown.

11. For his arms, take a black triple band and wrap them around your hook three times. Attach a white double band to the

hook, and slide the knot down over the white band. Slide this up the hook, and then attach a red band to the hook.

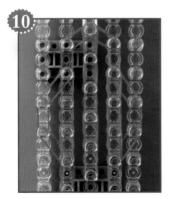

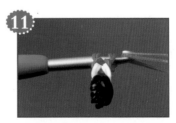

12. Slide the white and black knot over the red double bands. Repeat this twice to create his arm.

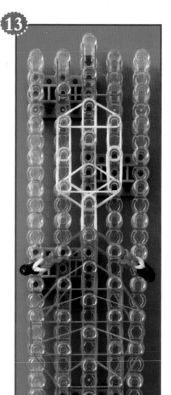

13. Attach his arms to the loom at the shoulders. To secure the figure, you will place a series of triangular crossover bands. Do this as seen in the photo, for a total of seven crossover bands.

14. Thread two black beads over a white band to create the eyes and attach to his face.

Looping:

1. Begin with Santa's boots. Do not loop the white "puffs" at his feet; hold the white bands while you loop the red. Loop all the bands in the belly except the center column, starting with the outside columns.

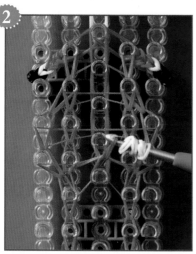

2. As you loop the center column of his belly, you will add the white puffs in his coat. Wrap a white double band around your hook. Do this one more time. With the white bands on your hook, start to unloop

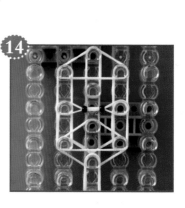

the next red band in the center column. Before you loop it back to the peg where it started, slide the white bands down onto the red band, and then secure it on the peg. Repeat this to the top of his suit or for a total of four puffs.

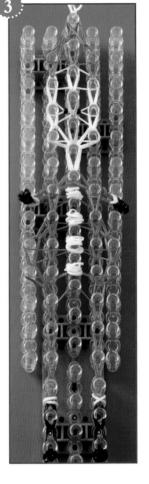

3. Loop the rest of the project until the top red bands. Pull the two red outside bands to the top center peg to create the peak of his hat. Using your hook, knot a white double band at the very last peg.

4. Remove the project from the loom very carefully.

To Make the Belt and Beard:

1. Wrap two black bands around his belly. Take a single gold band and hook it through his belt.

2. Pull the gold band through the body to his back and secure with a c-clip. Repeat this process for his buttons, but using single black bands up the white of his coat.

3. Take a single white band and feed it from the back of his head to the front of his face for half a mustache.

4. Keeping it on the hook, feed it through one of the white bands in side of his head. Take

another single white band and attach it to the end of the hook, as shown.

5. Pull this band through the bands in his face.

6. Knot the band on itself. Extend the band by feeding a new band through it and knotting it in the same way.

7. Loop another single band over your hook three times. Do this until your band is full, and attach to the band on Santa's face.

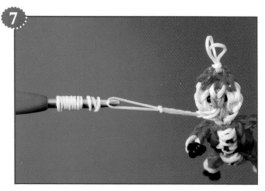

8. Slide the loops down onto the band from the hook to form the beard. Like you did with the first part of the mustache, feed another white band through his face, knot it, and feed it through a white band in the side of his face. Attach the beard, adding extension bands if necessary.

9. Using the extension bands, repeat the same process as the beard to create the puff in his hat. To secure, feed the end of the puff through the side of his head. Secure this band to the c-clip in the back of his

body, threading through other bands
if necessary so the body doesn't
bend.

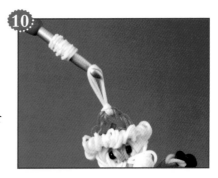

10. To make the pompom in his hat,
    wrap a band three times around your
    hook; repeat twice. Grab the white
    loop at the top of Santa's hat with
    this hook.

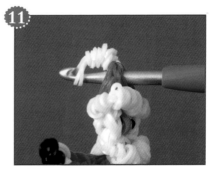

11. Slide these bands onto the loop.
    Feed your hook through the base of
    Santa's hat and grab the top of the
    white loop.

12. Pull the loop back through the base
    of Santa's hat.

13. Then wrap the loop over the top of the pompom to secure it.

SUPERHERO

What's that flying through the air? It's your own superhero, here to make your day! Swap out the colors to make him however you'd like. You can even make a whole team to help him fight crime! If you have only one loom, you can still make this project: just make the arms first, then loop and remove them from the loom. Before you loop your superhero, place the arms onto the shoulders. His shoulders won't be as wide and muscular when you build him this way.

Difficulty level: **Medium**

You need:

1 loom • 1 hook • 1 c-clip • black, blue, red, peach, and white bands • 1 clear band

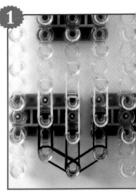

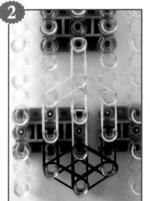

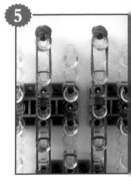

Set up your loom with five columns, offset: pull the outside and center columns one peg closer to you.

To Make Your Hero:

1. Attach black double bands to the first middle peg, and connect them to the left. Repeat and connect them to the right. Attach another pair of black bands, and attach them to the next middle peg. Lay double bands down the three middle columns, as shown, starting with black bands, then using different bands for your superhero's face, in this case peach.

2. Place diagonal black double bands from the first outside pegs to the second middle peg to finish off his hair. Place diagonal peach double bands from the third outside pegs to the fourth center peg. Connect three bands to the fourth middle peg, and connect them to the next middle peg.

3. Lay diagonal lines of blue triple bands from the neck to the sixth outside peg on both sides. Lay a line of blue double bands down the center column, ending on the fourth peg from the end.

4. Lay a line of blue double bands down the columns on either side of the center. Use red bands for the last two sets of bands.

5. Wrap three red bands around your hook three times, then thread

them through three red
bands. Put all the loops
from the last red bands
on your hook, then put it
onto the red "boot" band
at the end of the loom.
Repeat, and place the
other foot on the other
red boot.

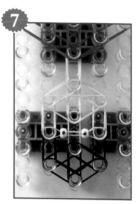

6. Lay double blue bands
down the outside
columns for the arms.
Wrap two peach
bands around your
hook three times, then
thread them through
another two peach
bands. Place the hands
onto the pegs at the
end of the arms, as
you did with the feet.

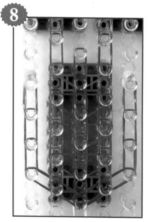

7. Thread two white beads onto a single peach
band, then attach it to the second row. Use a
marker to draw on his pupils. Place a single peach
band onto the third row in a triangle shape.

8. Place a single blue band across the sixth row
(just below his shoulders) in a triangle shape. Wrap a blue band
around your hook twice, and attach it to the seventh row in a triangle
shape. Do the same across the next two rows.

9. Turn your loom around and loop your bands back to where they
started. Make sure that where you laid out three bands you are also

looping back three bands. Secure the final loose loops with a clear band pulled through itself like a slipknot.

10. Remove your superhero from the loom and set him aside.

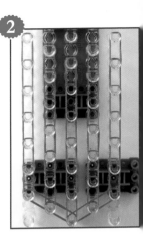

To Make the Cape:

1. Lay a diagonal line of red double bands from the first center peg to the second outside peg, first laying out the left side, then doing the same on the right.

2. Lay a line of red double bands down each column on your loom, ending on the seventh peg for the three center columns and the eighth peg for the outside columns.

3. Lay a single red band across each row, as shown.

4. Pull the horizontal bands at the bottom up and past the last middle peg.

5. Turn your loom around and loop your bands back to where they started. Secure the final loose loops with a double red band, and remove your cape from the loom.

6. Use your hook to pull single bands through your superhero to make his mouth and a chest emblem. Secure the bands to a single c-clip on his back.

7. Slide the loops from his cape over his neck to finish your superhero!

FEiSTY FiSH

Whether you love goldfish, the rowdy beta, or fascinating tropical navigators, this fish will go right along with any school in your loom collection! The body of the fish is simple to make, but the fins can get a little tricky, as you will be looping bands almost as if you are knitting. Once you have this down, you will have your fish friend in no time!

Difficulty level: **Easy**

You need:

1 loom • 2 hooks • 2 beads • 1 threader • rubber bands of different colors

Set up your loom horizontally and so that the center column is offset by one peg. You will use two different colors to create double bands. All bands are double, unless otherwise mentioned.

1. Using your double bands, lay out the figure shown. The white band is a triple band and will be where the eyes go.

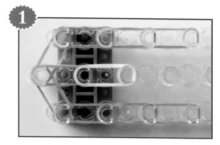

2. Thread a clear single band through two black beads for the eyes. Unhook one side of the white triple band from the loom, and place one side of the clear single band down. Replace the white bands, weave the clear single band through its center, and secure it to the loom.

3. Lay out the rest of the fish body, as shown.

4. To make the fins, you will create a bundle of knots. First, wrap a single band around your hook and slide it onto another single band.

5. Wrap another knot on your hook, and slide it onto the bundle you just made, reattaching the bundle to your hook afterward.

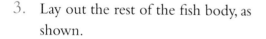

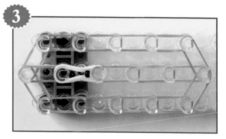

6. Wrap a band on itself once. Slide the bundle of bands onto this band.

7. Slide this bundle onto another single band, knotting it.

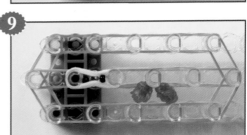

8. Repeat this process to make a second fin. Unhook one of the double bands from the loom, and attach the first fin.

9. Replace the double band that you moved over the first fin. Attach the second fin.

10. Wrap single bands once onto your hook, alternating colors and repeating until the hook is full. Slide these onto a double band and then reattach to the hook.

11. Slide this bundle onto another double band, and stretch the band across the pegs at the top of the fish's body.

12. For the big fin, wrap a double band around your hook and slide it onto another double band until you have two bundles. Slide one side of one of these bundles onto another double band, switching up your colors if you like.

13. Move this new bundle back onto your hook.

14. Repeat this process to make several bundles, keeping them all connected.

15. Slide the entire bundle onto a new double band, knotting this one so that you have a full fin.

16. Place the big fin at the end of the fish's body on the loom.

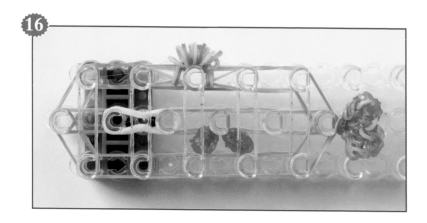

17. Loop the bands back to the pegs where they started, beginning with the tail of the fish and working left. Tie off the project with a band before removing it from the loom.

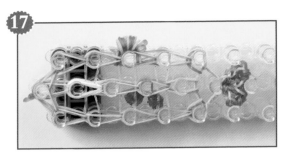

PRINCESS

Celebrate your loom fun with these beautiful fairy princesses! This project requires one loom and two additional columns for the princess' hair and dresses. If you only have one loom, you can make some of these parts off the loom and then connect them before you loop. You could also pool looms with a friend and make matching princesses together!

Difficulty level: **Medium**

You need:

1 loom + 2 columns • 1 hook • 1 c-clip • 2 beads • various colors of rubber bands for the hair, face, dress, and tiara

Set up your loom with the arrows facing toward you and the center column offset away from you. Attach one column on either side of the loom. All bands are double bands unless otherwise mentioned.

1. Lay out double bands for the hair and face. The band for her neck should be a triple band. Knit a short chain (one knot slid over two sets of double bands) for each of her pigtails, and attach to the ends of her hair.

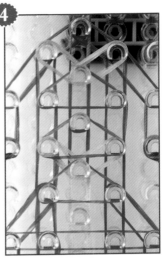

2. Lay out the princess's body, as shown. You will need to switch between colors for her skin, her dress, and the accent on her dress. Like her pigtails, make very short chains to add for her hands and feet.

3. Lay out single crossover bands across her dress. The band at the bottom should tuck behind the last center peg.

4. For her torso, lay out three single triangle crossover bands that have been wrapped once on themselves so they are taut.

5. Thread beads over a band for her eyes and attach to her face. Attach a single triangle crossover band over her face. Then, stretch two crossover bands wide across her face.

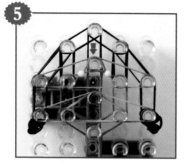

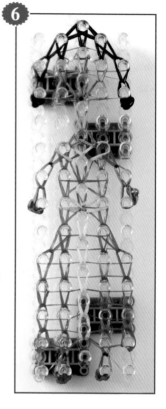

6. Starting from her shoes, loop the project back all the way up to the top. When looping the skirt and the arms, loop the outside first and work your way in. Make sure to remember to loop the accent in the middle of her dress, as well as the accent at her shoulders. Secure the project with a rubber band at the top.

7. Carefully remove the princess from the loom. Thread a pink band through her face for her lips and secure it behind her head. Form a short chain with gold bands and thread that through her hair to make a tiara, securing it at the back of her head as well. Use a marker to draw pupils in her eyes.

ROBOT

R2-who? Like no robot you've ever seen, this amazing bionic cyclops will be the coolest addition to your loom fun! Attach him to your backpack, glue him to a refrigerator magnet, or line him up with a whole army of robots! Our robot is silver, but the step-by-step photos are shown in bright green for better viewing. Metallic bands tend to be very thick, so be careful throughout your looming process to prevent them from snapping. While these instructions show how to create the robot in one loom with two columns, it is no problem if you only have one loom! The extra columns are for the arms, which can be done separately and then added to the figure. Now get in touch with your cyborg side and get cracking on this awesome project!

Difficulty level: **Medium**

You need:

1 loom **or** 1 loom + 2 columns • 1 regular hook • 1 fine hook • 6 beads • 1 googly eye • 1 flat-top button • silver and white bands

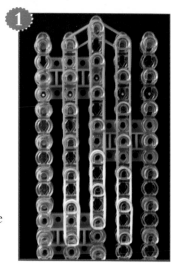

Set the loom up so that the arrows are pointing toward you. The center column should be offset by one peg moved away from you. All the bands will be double bands.

1. Using silver and white bands, lay out the shape, as shown. Use silver bands where we've put the green bands.

2. Continue laying your line of double bands down the columns next to the center, switching back to silver bands. These are his legs.

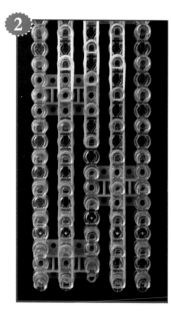

3. For his feet, create a triple band and wrap it around your hook twice so it looks like a knot. Take another triple band, and attach to the end of your hook, as shown.

4. Slide the knotted bands onto the center of the triple band, like in the photo.

5. Wrap it around the very bottom left peg in the loom to make his foot. Repeat this again for his right foot.

6. To make the body sturdier, you will create three triangles out of single silver bands called crossover bands. Starting

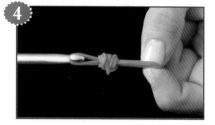

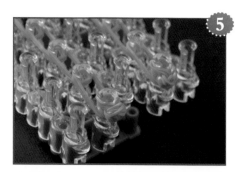

from the very bottom peg in the center column (where the body ends and the legs begin), wrap a crossover band around this peg and the two pegs below it on the left and right, so it looks like a triangle. Going up the body, make two more triangles, like in the photo.

7. For his computer, slide three beads onto your fine hook. Attach a white single band to the end of your hook, and slide the beads over the band. Stretch the band a little and attach it across the white pegs in the middle of his body. Do this with two beads for the row above, as shown. If your beads do not fit over the hook, see the section in our glossary on bead threading.

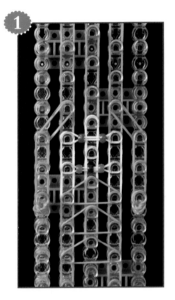

To Make the Arms:

If you have just one loom, you will need to make the arms separately and then attach them to the fourth pegs in the left and right columns. The following photos show the project using extra columns.

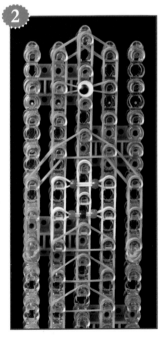

1. Attach silver double bands diagonally to the outside columns from his shoulders (the fourth pegs on the right and left columns), and then create the arms like in the photo. To make the hands, repeat steps 3 through 5 with double bands instead of triple, and attach them to the bottom of his arms.

2. Attach a single crossover band at the shoulders to connect the arms. For the eye, use a googly eye bead or a bead with a flat face and glue a googly eye to the bead.

Thread a single silver band through the eye, and attach it to the face, as shown.

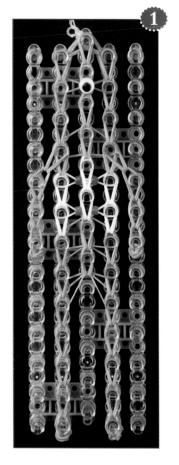

Looping:

1. Start with the feet. Hold the feet down so they do not come unattached from the pegs, and loop the bands back to the pegs where they originated. Do the legs first, then the body, and then the arms and head. When you reach the first crossover band at the top of his legs, tuck this band up behind the center peg. You will loop this with the bands on the bottom peg in the center column. At the top of the robot's head, tie a band through the top band and pull it tight to knot it.

2. Gently remove the project from the loom.

To Make the Mask:

1. Knit a single chain or fishtail stitch in white bands.

2. Wrap the mask over the robot's face, making sure to snugly secure the bands around the googly eye. Secure the mask behind the robot's head with an s- or c-clip.

GARDEN GNOME

Whether he hides in your garden or hangs off your backpack, this garden gnome is awesome. This project requires an extended loom because his body is wide. If you do not have access to extra columns, you can make the sides of his body off the loom, loop them, and then attach the sides to the regular loom before you loop the rest of the body back. (To see this process in action, please refer to the Medusa project on page 215.) Now get gnoming!

Difficulty level: **Medium**

You need:

1 loom or 1 loom + 2 columns • 1 hook • 1 c-clip • 2 black beads • red, green, black, gray, orange, and white bands

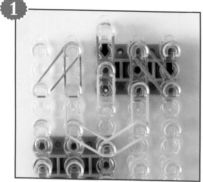

Set up your loom so the center column is offset one peg away from you. Attach one column on either side of the loom. All bands are double bands unless otherwise mentioned.

1. Lay out red and orange double bands for the first part of his head, as shown.

2. Continue by laying out white double bands for his beard.

3. Start his torso with black and green double bands.

4. Make his pants with gray double bands.

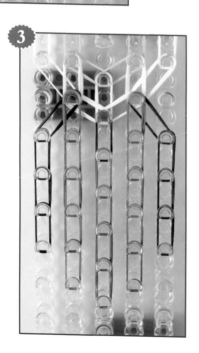

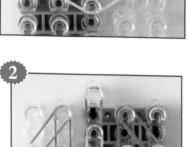

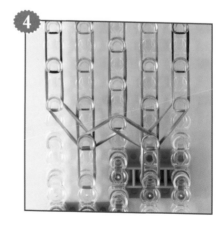

5. Attach black triple bands for his feet. Wrap a black double band around your hook and slide it onto another black triple band and attach it to the loom for the sole of his shoe.

6. Using orange and black double bands, knit two chains for his arms and attach them to the loom at his shoulders. Stretch four single gray crossover bands over his torso.

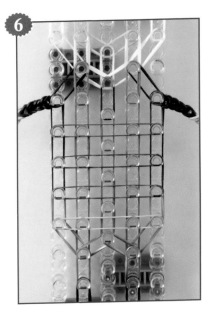

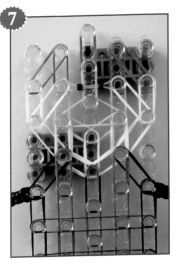

7. Attach an orange crossover band to the gnome's face, and add eyes by threading a single clear band through two black beads.

8. Create four separate knots by wrapping a red double band around your hook and sliding it over another red double band. Slide all of these onto one red double band, and knot it together to make a bouquet.

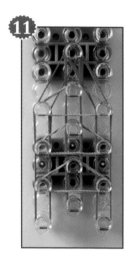

9. Wrap it with a green double band and pull it through the gnome's hand.

10. Loop the bands back very carefully. When doing the torso, loop the outside columns first (including the shoulders), then the inside. Secure the red bands at the top. This will be temporary while you make his hat.

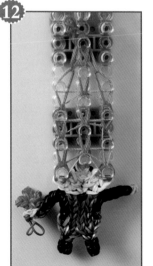

11. Using a regular loom with the center column offset, build his hat with red double bands. Attach single crossover bands to the loom; these should be wrapped once on themselves so that they are taut.

12. Knit a short chain of red double bands, and attach it to the very top of his hat. Attach his body to the bottom of the hat. Starting

from the bottom of the hat, loop the bands back to the pegs where they started, going all the way up to the pointy part in his hat. Secure with a red double band or a c-clip and remove from the loom.

13. Wrap several single bands individually onto your hook. Slide them onto an extended single band to create the puffs in his beard (several single bands knotted together to make one long band). Attach the beard to his face by threading the ends through his hair and tying it at the back. To make the beard longer, repeat this process but attach the extension to the bottom of his beard. This will also help secure his beard to the bottom of his face.

CAT

This friendly feline is perfect for your loom menagerie! While the ears can be a little tricky to loop because the bands are tightly wrapped, the rest of this project is super easy to put together. Play a game of cat and mouse with the other creatures in this book, or let this kitten purr on its own!

Difficulty level: **Easy**

You need:

1 loom • 1 hook • black, white, and pink bands

To Make the Ears:

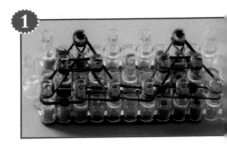

1. Set up your loom horizontally, with the center column offset toward the left. Using single black bands that have been wrapped once on themselves, lay out two triangles that are connected by a band in between. Add a triple-wrapped crossover band to each triangle. Add a cap band that has been wrapped five times to both top points of the triangles.

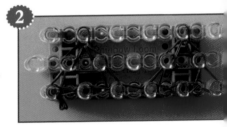

2. Loop back by starting from the points and working down. Loop the long bottom row of bands last, starting from the far right and moving to the far left. Before removing from the loom, tie a double-wrapped single band (in a slipknot) to both ends of the project to secure it. You will need these when you attach the ears to the body.

To Make the Body:

1. Now, set up your loom vertically with the arrows facing toward you (and the center column still offset). Lay out the body of the cat using all double bands, except for the neck, where it will be a triple band. The white feet at the bottom should have cap bands that have been wrapped three times.

2. Make a long single chain with about six black double bands for the tail.

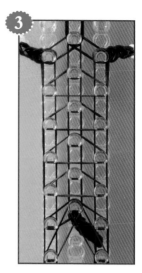

Make two shorter single chains—starting with white double bands and then switching to black—for the front legs. Attach the tail, legs, and ears to the loom where shown.

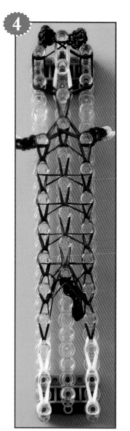

3. Lay out four triangle crossover bands over the cat's belly. The bottom one should be wrapped once on itself so that it is tighter. Then, attach a band diagonally on either side of the tail and another two bands stretched diagonally to just below the tail.

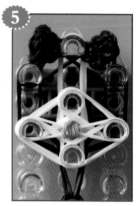

4. Starting from the feet, loop the bands back up until you reach the chin. Do not loop any farther than this just yet.

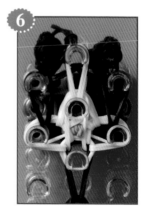

5. Make the muzzle on your cat's face by attaching white double bands in a diamond shape. Then, slide a wrapped pink single band over a white single band, and stretch it across the muzzle.

6. Starting from the bottom of the muzzle, carefully loop the bands back. Save the top white band for last, and then tie the project off at the top.

7. Carefully pull the cat off the loom. Using your hook, pull four black rubber bands through the pink nose, and then snip the ends of the black bands to make the cat's whiskers. To make the cat stand upright, pull his front paws through a band or two on the edges of his torso.

LADYBUG

Did you know ladybugs are also called ladybirds? What do you call these little beetles? Ladybugs are happiest in a garden, so why not make some flowers to keep her company!

Difficulty level: **Easy**

You need:

1 loom • 1 hook • red and black bands

Set up your loom offset, with the middle column pulled one closer to you and the arrow pointing away.

1. Attach two black bands to the first middle peg, and connect them to the next middle peg. Attach another pair of black bands to the first middle peg, and connect them to the peg to the right. Attach another pair of black bands, and connect them to the next peg to the left.

2. Lay a line of double red bands down the middle column, ending on the fifth peg.

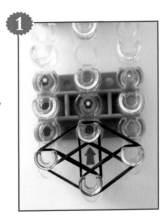

3. Lay a hexagon shape onto the loom using double red bands. Lay out the left side and then the right.

4. Attach two red bands to the third middle peg, then connect them to the next peg to the right. Attach another pair of bands and connect them to the next peg on the left. Do the same with the fourth middle peg.

5. Wrap a black band around your hook three times, and thread it onto a single red band. Repeat to make five total "spots" for your ladybug.

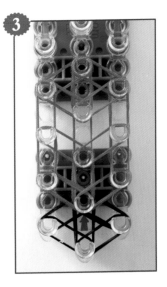

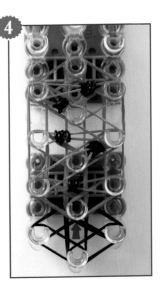

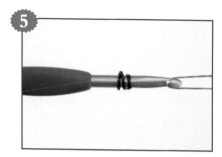

6. Place the bands from your spots onto the loom, as shown.

7. Turn your loom, and begin looping your bands back to where they started. Loop any red diagonal bands back to the center. Loop the first set of black diagonal bands from the center out, and loop the second set of black diagonal bands in to the center.

8. Pull a black band through the loose loops on the last peg, and pull one end of the band through the other like a slipknot.

9. Remove your ladybug from the loom. Knot your finishing loop again, then cut it at the end, and tie a knot at the end of each strand to make the antenna.

PEGASUS

Fly away with this amazing project! This delightful stallion has the best of both fantasy steeds: a sparkly horn like a unicorn and powerful wings like the ancient mythological Pegasus. Your Pegasus will require a few intricate steps, but the outcome is absolutely adorable!

Difficulty level: **Hard**

You need:

1 loom • 1 hook • 2 beads • sparkly, pink, white, and black bands

To Make the Legs:

1. Starting on the eighth peg from the end, lay
   a line of four sets of double pink bands down
   the left column. Wrap a white band around
   your hook twice, and attach it to the next two
   pegs. Repeat to lay doubled white bands down
   the rest of the column. Wrap a black cap band
   around the last peg three times, then repeat
   with a second cap band.

2. To finish the front legs, loop your bands back to
   where they started and remove your leg from
   the loom. For the back legs, attach double pink
   bands to the sixth and seventh pegs from the
   end in the middle column.

3. Loop your leg as usual until you
   reach the second to last pink peg.
   Instead of looping this band back
   to where it started, loop it to the
   sixth peg from the end in the
   middle column.

4. Continue looping your back leg
   and remove it from the loom.
   Make two front legs and two back legs.

To Make the Wings:

1. Lay single sparkly bands down the center column, ending on the
   third peg. Lay out a half hexagon shape on the left side using single
   sparkly bands, ending on the third middle peg.

2. Lay a line of single sparkly bands up the right column, ending on the
   fifth peg.

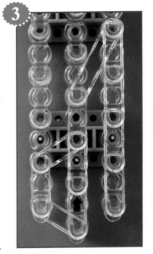

3. Attach a single band to the third middle peg, and connect it to the next middle peg. Attach a single sparkly band to the fourth middle peg, and connect it to the fifth peg on the right. Wrap a cap band around the fifth peg in the right column.

4. Wrap a sparkly band around your hook twice, and place it on the second row in a triangle shape. Wrap another band around your hook twice, and place it on the right and middle columns, as shown.

5. Turn your loom around and loop your wing. Place the loose loops from the final two pegs on your hook and thread them onto two sparkly bands. Repeat to make a second wing.

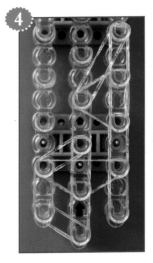

To Make the Whole Body:

1. Use pink double bands to lay a hexagon shape onto the loom. Lay down the right side, then the left.

2. Stack white bands on the first middle peg (we used about ten). Attach two white bands to the first middle peg, and connect them to the next middle peg. Push the white bands onto this band. Repeat with the next peg, using pink double bands between the second and third peg.

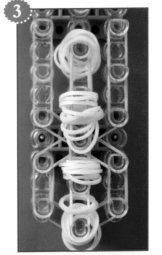

3. Attach a single pink band to the third middle peg, and connect it to the left.

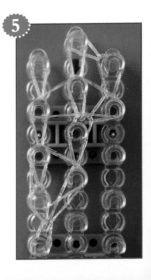

Repeat on the right. Lay a line of single pink bands down the outside columns, ending on the fifth peg. Stack white bands on the fourth middle peg as you did before. Attach three pink bands to the third middle peg, and connect it to the next middle peg. Move the white bands onto the three pink bands. Repeat on the next peg.

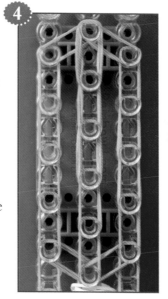

4. Starting at the fifth middle peg, use pink double bands to lay out a long hexagon shape. Lay a line of pink double bands down the center of the hexagon.

5. Put all the end loops from your wings onto your hook, then thread them onto a single pink band. Place the pink band onto the second row of your hexagon, in a triangle shape. Tuck the wings down into the loom.

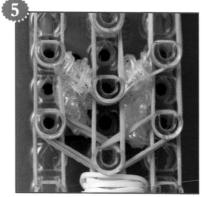

6. Wrap a pink band around your hook three times, then thread it onto pink double bands. Put both ends of the pink double bands on your hook, then put the loops onto the first peg on the left. Repeat, and place the other loop on the right.

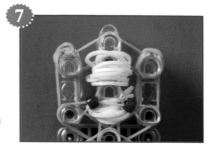

7. Thread two beads onto a single pink band, and attach it to the second row on the loom, in a triangle shape.

8. Place your back legs on the last two pegs in the outside columns.

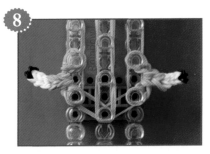

9. Place a single pink band around the pegs in the second row in a triangle shape. Wrap a pink band around the third row two times (or three times, if you can stretch it enough). Wrap a pink band around your hook twice, then attach it to the fourth row in a triangle shape. Place double pink bands across the seventh and eighth rows in a triangle shape.

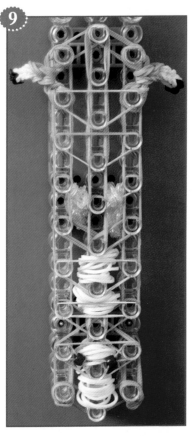

10. Wrap a gold sparkly band around your hook three times. Thread it onto gold sparkly double bands. Use your hook to "knit" a chain four loops long with the wrapped band at the end. Thread the last gold loops through a single pink band and place it on the first row.

11. Turn your loom around and begin looping the outside columns. When you reach the diagonal bands in the fifth row (right after the wings), thread

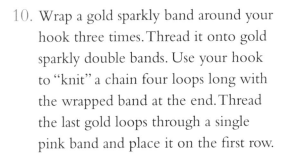

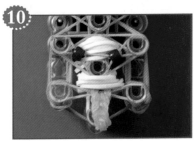

one of the front legs onto your hook, then thread it onto the diagonal band before you loop it back to the middle peg. Do the same on the other side with the other leg.

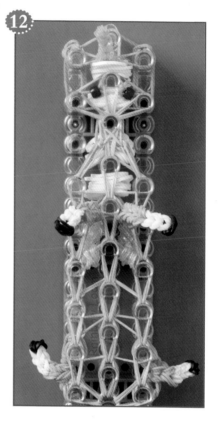

12. Loop the middle pegs, then continue looping the rest of the pegs, ending at the third peg from the end.

13. Lay a line of pink double bands down the center column from the second peg to the fourth. Attach double pink bands to the second peg from the end in the outside columns, and connect them to the third peg. Wrap a pink band around your hook twice. Attach it to the third peg from the end in the outside column, and connect it to the next middle peg. Do the same on the other side.

14. Wrap a pink band around your hook twice, and place it across the second row in a triangle shape. Wrap a pink band around your hook three times, and attach it to the third row. Wrap a pink cap band around the fourth middle peg three times.

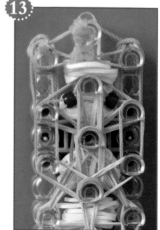

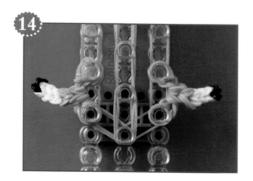

15. Starting at the fourth middle peg, begin looping your Pegasus's face. Before you loop the last three pegs at the top, add a bundle of single white bands to the top center peg; this will be the top of Pegasus's mane. Loop the rest of the bands back as normal to secure the mane. Tie off the project at the top with a rubber band before you remove it from the loom.

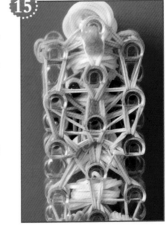

16. To add Pegasus's ponytail, slide a bundle of white single bands over another single band and attach it to the loom. Do this two more times so they are all connected.

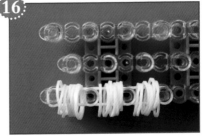

17. Loop the tail back (you do not need a cap band). Remove it from the loom.

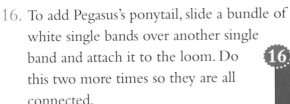

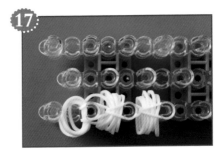

Attach the tail to the end of the project by weaving the loose bands through a pink band and tying everything off with a slipknot. You can wrap the loop of the slipknot over the tail to secure.

DUCK

Make your own rubberband duckie! This project is perfect for a rainy day inside or any time you want a happy little yellow bird to brighten your day. Or you can make a whole flock in a rainbow of colors!

Difficulty level: **Easy**

You need:

1 loom • 1 hook • 1 c-clip • yellow and orange bands • 2 black bands

Set up your loom offset, with the middle pegs pulled one peg closer to you.

To Make the Wings and Tail Feathers:

1. Lay a line of double bands down a column, ending on the fourth peg for the wings, as shown, and the third peg for the tail feather pieces. Triple-loop a yellow cap band around the last peg in your line.

2. Turn your loom around. Starting with the peg with the cap band, begin looping your bands back to the peg where they started.

3. Carefully remove your chain from the loom and set aside.

4. Repeat to make two wings and two tail feather pieces.

To Make the Beak:

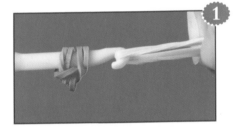

1. Wrap an orange band onto your hook three times. Use your hook to "knit" a chain *two* loops long (one orange, one yellow) with the orange band on the end.

2. Set your beak aside.

To Make the Head and Body:

1. Attach two yellow bands to the first middle peg, and connect them to the first peg on the left.

2. Lay out a long hexagon shape onto the loom, as shown. Lay out the left side, then the right side of the shape.

3. Pick up your beak. Attach one end of the yellow band to the third peg on the left and the other end to the third peg on the right.

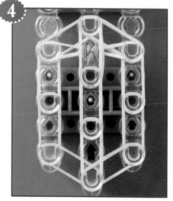

4. Lay a line of double bands down the center of your hexagon.

5. To make the eyes, wrap two black bands separately around your hook three times. Thread them both onto a single yellow band.

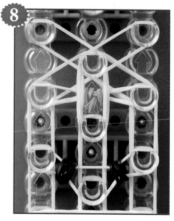

6. Attach the yellow band with your bird's eyes to the second peg on the right and left. Use your hook to pull the middle of the yellow band down to attach it to the second middle peg. Make sure the black "eye" bands are on either side of the middle peg.

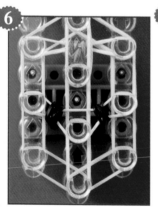
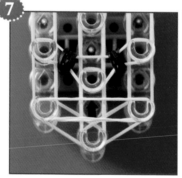
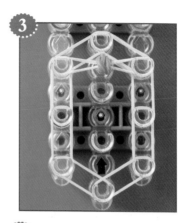

7. Wrap a single band around the bottom right and left pegs twice, as a cap band.

8. Attach a single yellow band to the fourth middle peg, and connect it to the next peg to the left. Attach another single yellow band to the middle peg, and connect it to the right.

9. Lay a long hexagon shape onto the loom, as you did with the head shape. Lay the left side of the shape first, then the right side.

10. Lay out a line of double bands down the center column of your long hexagon shape.

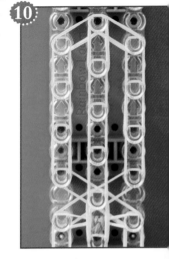

Putting It Together:

1. Take one of the wings, remove the c-clip, and use your hook to slide all four loops onto the fourth peg on the left.

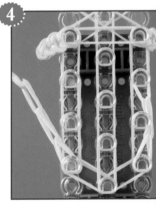

2. Do the same for the other wing, attaching it to the fourth peg on the right.

3. Attach two yellow bands to the fourth peg on the right, and connect the other end to the fourth peg on the left (where you attached the wings).

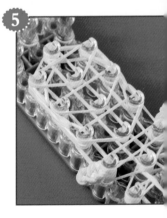

4. Attach the tail feather pieces to your bird: Remove the c-clip and slide all four loops onto the last peg on the left. Grab the other end of the tail feather chain and attach the loop at the end to the fifth peg on the left. Do the same on the right side.

5. Attach two yellow bands to the fifth middle peg and the fifth pegs on the right and left to make a triangle shape. Repeat for the sixth and

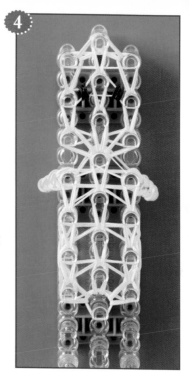

seventh rows, making a triangle shape for each. Wrap a cap band three times onto the last middle peg in your shape.

Looping:

1. Turn your loom around, and starting with the middle peg closest to you, begin looping your bands back onto the pegs where they started.

2. Loop the pegs along the left side of your body shape, then the right. Then, loop the middle bands of the body shape, ending at the middle "neck" peg.

3. From the fifth middle peg (the "neck"), loop all the bands off that peg, first to the middle, then to the left, then to the right. Continue looping the head circle shape as you did the body, first looping the left outside pegs, then the right, then the middle column.

4. Secure the loose loops on the final peg with a single band or with a c-clip, then carefully remove your bird from the loom.

To Add the Feet:

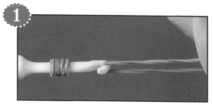

1. Wrap an orange band around your hook four times. Stretch another orange band between the hook and your finger.

2. Thread the looped band onto the stretched orange band. Pull one end of the single band through the other and pull it snug.

3. Put your hook though the back of your bird, through the four loops at the bottom corner, and grab the remaining loop from your bird's foot. Pull the loop through, then pull the foot through the loop to secure it.

4. Repeat to make the second foot.

DOG

What a good dog! This little Fido can sit and stay where you put him, and he can even roll over (with a little bit of help)! Make him your best friend, or craft a whole pack to keep him company!

Difficulty level: **Easy**

You need:

1 loom • 1 hook • 1 c-clip • white, black, and red bands

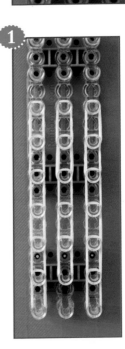

Set up your loom with the pegs square and the arrow pointing away from you.

To Make the Snout:

1. Lay single bands across the first row, moving from left to right. Lay two sets of double bands up the right and left columns, then one pair down the middle.

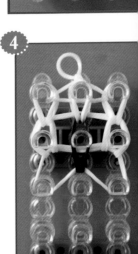

2. Wrap a black band onto your hook three times. Use your hook to thread it onto two black bands. Attach one end of the double black bands to the second middle peg and the other end to the third middle peg. This is your dog's nose.

3. Attach two white bands across the second row. Do the same on the third row. Pull the middle of the bands across the third row off the middle peg.

4. Turn your loom around. Loop the pegs along the left side, then the right, and then the middle column.

5. Secure the loose loops from the final peg with a single band and remove the snout from the loom.

To Make the Face:

1. Lay out a line of white double bands up all three columns, ending on the seventh peg. Skip the first peg in the middle column.

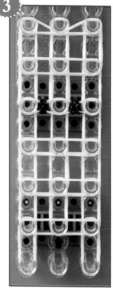

2. Wrap two black bands separately onto your hook three times. Thread the two black bands onto a single white band. Attach the white band for your dog's eyes to the fifth row. Make sure the black bands are separated.

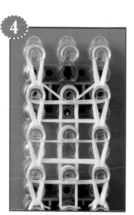

3. Lay white double bands across the second, third, and fourth rows. Skip the fifth row with your dog's eyes, then lay double bands across the sixth and seventh rows in the same way. Pull the bands in the last row toward you, as shown.

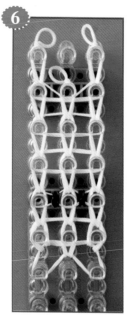

4. Turn your loom around. Loop the pegs on the left side of the loom, then loop the right side. Use your hook to pull the middle of the bands across what is now the second-to-last row toward you, as shown.

5. Loop the middle column.

6. Secure the loose loops on each of the three last pegs with a single band. Remove your dog's face from the loom.

To Add the Snout:

1. Use your hook to pull a white band halfway through your snout, in the same center loop where the black band runs through.

2. Pull both ends of the white band through to the back of the dog's face, and secure the ends with a c-clip.

To Make the Legs:

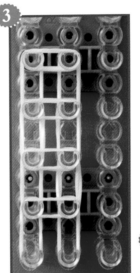

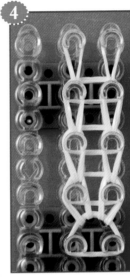

1. Attach a single band to the first two pegs in each the left and middle columns.

2. Lay out a line of white bands down the left and middle columns, ending on the fifth peg. Use single bands to connect rows 1 and 2 and double bands for the rest.

3. Wrap a white cap band twice around the middle and left pegs in rows 2 through 5. You can add an additional double-looped band on the fifth row to make your dog stand better.

4. Turn your loom around and loop your bands back to where they started. Do not loop the horizontal bands.

5. Remove from the loom. Repeat three more times to make your dog's four legs.

To Make the Body:

1. Attach a band to the fifth peg on the left, then connect it to the next peg up and the next peg to the right to make a triangle.

2. Thread the loops from one of your dog legs onto two white bands, and attach the bands to the left column above the triangle. Do the same on the right.

3. Lay a line of double white bands down the rest of the middle column and to the second-to-last peg on the left. Place your third dog leg onto the last two pegs on the left as you did before.

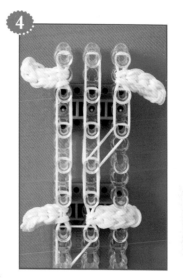

4. Attach a single band to the middle peg four from the end and connect it to the right column. Attach two bands to the peg where you ended your diagonal band, and connect it to the next peg in the right column. Attach your last dog leg to the final two pegs in the right column, as you did before.

5. Lay two white bands across the pegs in the last row. Do the same on the second-to-last row on the loom. Wrap a single band two times across the pegs in the third row from the end.

6. Wrap a single band two times across the left and middle pegs in the fourth row from the end. Do the same for the fifth and sixth rows from the end.

7. Either on your loom or using your hook, make a white single-loop chain five bands long for your dog's tail.

8. Thread the end loops of your tail onto your hook. Double-loop a single band and pull it tight between your hook and your finger. Thread the loops for your tail onto the double-looped band.

9. Attach the double-looped tail band to the left and middle pegs in the sixth row.

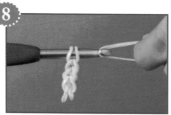

To Put It All Together:

1. Put your hook through a stitch

on the back of your dog's head piece, as shown. Pull a single white band partway through so the ends of the band hang off the back of the face. Do the same on the right side.

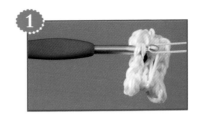

2. Attach both loops from the single bands onto the right and left pegs on the end of the loom. Turn your loom so the dog is facing you.

3. Pull the middle of the band across the first row off the middle peg.

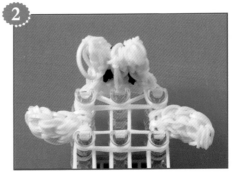

4. Starting at the peg closest to you on the left, begin looping your bands back. Loop the left column first, making sure to loop the diagonal band from the last peg back to the peg in the middle column. Then loop the bands in the right column, stopping after you loop the sixth peg. Loop the middle pegs next, stopping again after the sixth peg.

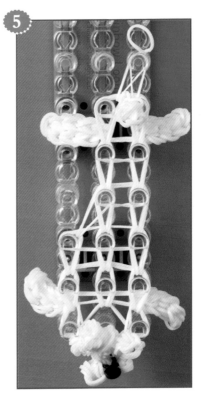

5. Pull your dog's tail toward you to move it out of the way, then loop your last two pegs. Then loop the band from the second-to-last peg on the right back to the last peg in the right column. Loop the single band from the last middle peg to the last peg in the right column.

6. Secure the loose loops on the final peg with a single band: pull the band through

the loops, then pull one end of the band through the other and pull it tight.

7. Remove your dog from the loom. Use your fingers to neaten up the bands and your hook to tuck in any leftover loops. Use your fingers to slide two red bands around your dog's neck for a collar.

SPiDeR

This creepy crawly spider isn't too scary, and it's a cinch to put together! This little arachnid fits in your pocket, and it makes a terrific handmade Halloween decoration!

Difficulty level: **Easy**

You need:

1 loom • 1 hook • 1 c-clip • black bands • 2 red bands

Set up your loom offset with the middle column pulled one peg closer to you.

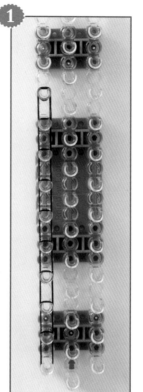

To Make the Legs:

1. Lay out a line of double bands up the left column, ending on the seventh peg for the short legs, and the tenth peg for the long legs, as shown. Wrap a black cap band onto the last peg three times.

2. Turn your loom around. Starting at the peg where you placed the cap band, loop your bands back to the pegs where they started.

3. Secure the loose bands with a c-clip for now and set aside.

4. Make six total short legs and two total long legs in this way.

To Make the Body:

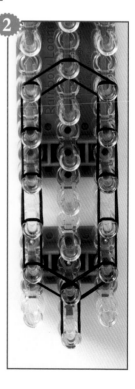

1. Attach two black bands to the first middle peg, then connect them to the next middle peg.

2. Starting on the second middle peg, lay out a long hexagon shape. Lay out the left side, then lay out the right side of the shape in the same way.

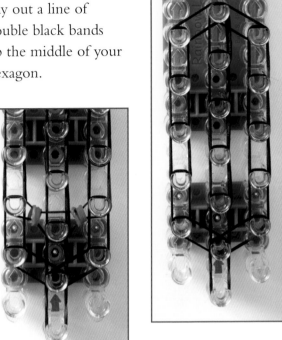

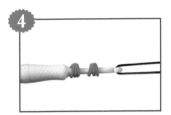

3. Lay out a line of double black bands up the middle of your hexagon.

4. Wrap two red bands around your hook three times. Thread your red bands onto a single black band. These will be your spider's eyes.

5. Attach your eye band to the third row of pegs, in a triangle shape.

6. Lay a single band in a triangle shape across the second, fourth, and fifth rows.

7. Wrap a cap band around the last middle peg three times.

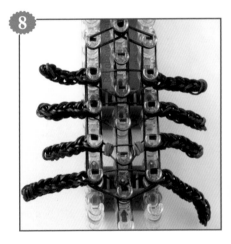

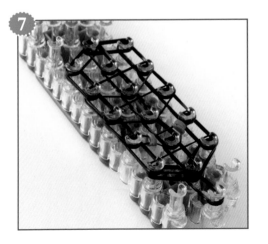

8. Add your spider legs: Remove the c-clip, and slide all four loose loops onto the pegs, as shown. Place the two long legs on the second pegs on the right and left.

9. Begin looping your bands back to where they started: Loop the closest middle peg first, then loop the left column, then the right. Loop the middle column last.

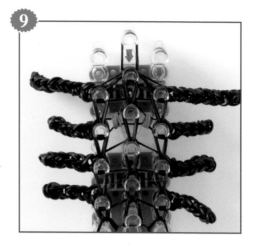

10. Finish your project by looping the single band from the second-to-last middle peg back to the last middle peg. Secure the loose loops with a c-clip or tie it off with a rubber band.

11. Remove your spider from your loom. Bend your spider's legs to make him stand!

PiG

Oink! Just like real pigs, this little piggy is smart: he can even stand up on his own! This project has a few pieces, but he's not too hard to put together!

Difficulty level: **Medium**

You need:

1 loom • 1 hook • pink, black, brown, and white bands

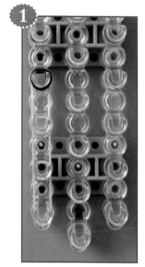

Set up your loom offset, with the center column pulled one closer to you and the arrow facing away.

1. Lay a line of pink bands down the left column, ending on the fourth peg. Wrap a black cap band around the fourth peg three times, then repeat with a second black cap band.

2. Turn your loom around and loop your bands back where they started. Repeat to make four legs for your pig.

3. Using pink double bands, lay out a hexagon shape onto the loom. Lay out the left side then the right.

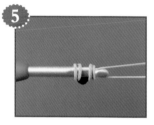

4. Lay a line of double pink bands down the center of your hexagon.

5. To make the snout, wrap a brown band around your hook three times, then thread it onto double pink bands. Put both ends of the pink bands onto your hook. Thread the pink bands and the brown band onto a single pink band. Set snout aside while you make the eyes.

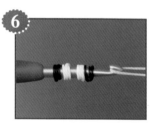

6. To make the eyes, wrap a black band around your hook three times. Do the same with a white band, then another white band, and finally another black band. Thread these onto a single pink band.

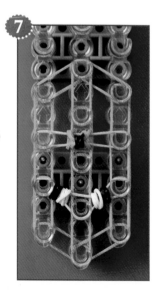

7. Place the single band with your snout onto the third row on the loom. Place the single band with your eye bands onto the second row in a triangle shape.

8. Wrap a pink band around your hook three times, then thread it onto a single pink band. Put both loops of the pink band onto your hook, then put them onto the first peg on the left. Repeat and place your second ear on the first right peg.

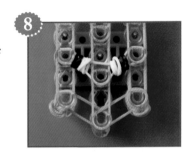

9. Wrap a pink band around your hook two times. Attach it to the first pegs on the right and left. Repeat and place your band across the fourth row in a triangle shape. Place two pink bands onto the third row in a triangle shape.

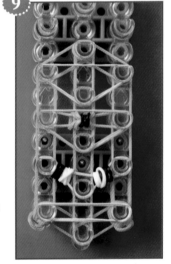

10. Turn your loom and loop your bands back to where they started. Loop the outside columns, then the center column. Pull a single pink band through the final loose loops: pull one end of the pink band through the other and pull it tight like a slipknot.

11. Remove your pig's face from the loom. Wrap a pink band around your hook twice, then slide it onto your pig's snout. Repeat with a second band.

12. Starting at the seventh middle peg from the
end, lay a line of double pink bands down
the center of your loom. Attach two pink
bands to the seventh middle peg from the
end, and connect them to the left; then
repeat and connect them to the right. Lay
a line of double bands down both outside
columns.

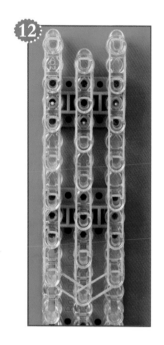

13. Place your pig's legs onto the corner pegs
of your shape.

14. Place two bands across the seventh row
from the end. Lay out double pink bands in
a triangle shape across the remaining rows
in your shape. Pull the triangle on the last
pegs in front of the last middle peg.

15. Use your hook to pull a single pink band
through the loops on the outside of your
pig's face. Do this on both sides of the face.

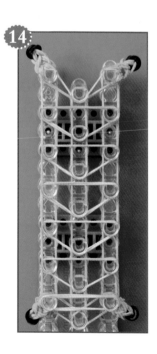

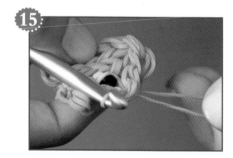

16. Place the loops on the outside pegs of the last row.

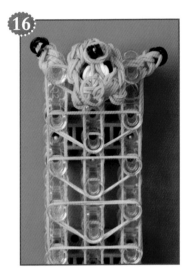

17. Turn your loom and loop your bands back to where they started. Tie off the last loose loops with a single pink band: pull one end of the band through the other to make a slipknot, then remove the pig from the loom.

BUNNY

Here comes Peter Rubberband-tail! This fluffy bunny can be made in a rainbow of colors. Make him as a festive springtime accessory or just about any time you need an extra bounce in your step.

Set up your loom offset, with the middle column pulled toward you one peg.

To Make the Arms:

1. Lay out a line of double bands along the left column, ending on the fourth peg. Wrap a white cap band onto the fourth peg three times.

2. Turn your loom around. Loop your bands back to the pegs where they started.

3. Secure the loose loops from the final peg with your hook, or with a c-clip, and remove the arm from the loom. Set it aside. Repeat to make your bunny's second arm.

To Make the Head:

1. Lay double bands in a hexagon shape onto your loom as shown, first laying out the left side, then the right.

2. Lay double bands down the middle of your hexagon, ending on the third peg.

3. Wrap a pink band onto your hook three times. Thread it onto two purple bands, and attach the bands to the second and third pegs in the middle column. This will be your bunny's mouth.

4. Wrap two separate black bands onto your hook three times. Thread the bands onto two purple bands, and attach the bands to the second row, making sure the black bands are pushed to either side.

5. Wrap a single band twice across each the first and third rows, as shown.

To Make the Ears:

1. Wrap a purple band around your hook three times. Thread it onto two purple bands, then wrap a white band around your hook three times. Place the end of your two purple bands onto the hook behind the white band.

2. Continue to "knit" in this way, threading the loops from your hook onto double purple bands, then adding a white band to the hook before putting the other end of the purple double band onto the hook. Knit a chain three loops long.

3. Stretch a single purple band between your hook and your finger, and slide the loops off the hook, threading them onto the single band.

4. Place your bunny ear onto the first peg in the left column. Repeat to make your second ear, and place it onto the first peg in the right column.

To Make the Body:

1. Attach a single purple band to the fourth middle peg, and connect it to the left. Attach another single band, and connect it to the right.

2. Lay out purple double bands in a long hexagon shape, as you did for the head. Lay out the left side first, then the right.

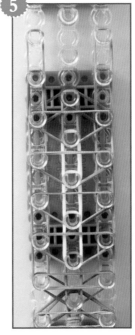

3. Lay a line of double bands down the middle of your body shape. Use purple bands for the first and last set of pegs and white bands in the middle.

4. Lay double bands down the right and left columns to make your bunny's legs.

5. Attach double bands to the fifth through the eighth rows in a triangle shape, as shown. Attach two purple bands to the fourth row.

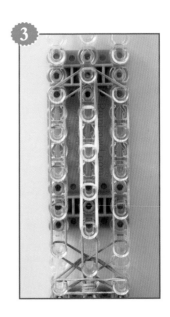

6. Place your bunny's arms on the right and left pegs in the fourth row.

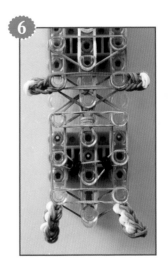

To Make the Tail:

1. Wrap five separate purple bands onto your hook two times. Thread them onto a single purple band.

2. Place it onto the last peg in your body shape.

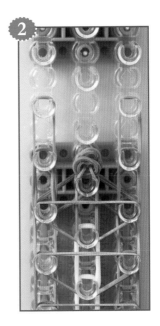

To Make the Feet:

1. Wrap a purple band onto your hook three times. Thread it onto two purple bands. Wrap a white band around the hook as you did for the ears, then put the other end of the purple bands back on the hook. Thread the purple and white bands onto two purple bands.

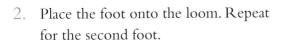

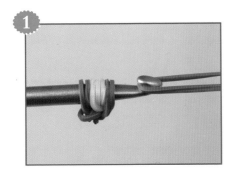

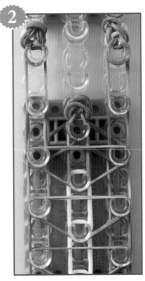

2. Place the foot onto the loom. Repeat for the second foot.

To Loop Your Bunny:

1. Turn your loom around. Loop your bunny's legs, then loop the middle peg with his tail. Loop the left side of the body shape, then the right, and then finally the middle column.

2. When you loop the middle "neck" peg, you should loop the middle peg first, then the one to the left, and, finally, the bands going to the right. Then finish looping the head shape as you did the body.

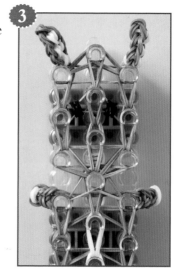

3. Secure the loose loops from the final peg with a c-clip or tie it off with a single band. Remove your bunny from the loom.

MEDUSA

Beware the terrifying and beautiful Greek Gorgon! Medusa was a mythological monster with live snakes for hair who could turn all those who stared at her to stone. Her name actually means "guardian," for her power to stop anyone in his tracks. We have shown how to make her wide dress using only one loom. If you have an extra loom, simply add one column on either side of her and lay out all the bands for the dress together. Now get rolling and make this super cool figure with all her slithering green snakes!

Difficulty level: **Medium**

You need:

1 loom • 1 hook • green, maroon, purple, red, black, and yellow bands

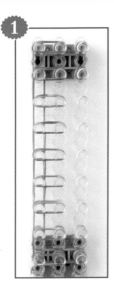

Set up your loom square so that all the columns are even. All the bands will be double bands, unless otherwise mentioned.

1. Lay out a line of purple double bands in the far left column and perpendicular bands along each row. This will be part of her dress. Loop these bands back, starting from the bottom (treat the last band as a cap band).

2. Repeat this process on the opposite column on the right side of the loom, with the perpendicular bands going left. Set these aside, and lay out her head and body, as shown.

3. Attach the purple bands that you set aside to the sides of the loom to widen her dress.

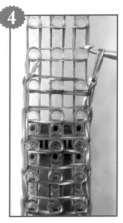

4. Place three separate crossover bands onto her torso (rows 4, 5, and 6 on the loom). To do this, wrap a single purple band on itself before stretching it across the loom. For the bottom crossover band, you will need to temporarily unhook the extra dress bands, attach the crossover band, and reattach the extra dress bands, as shown.

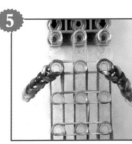

5. Make her arms by creating a chain of double bands using yellow, purple, and red bands and attach to the loom at her shoulders.

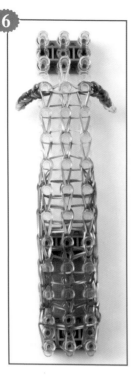

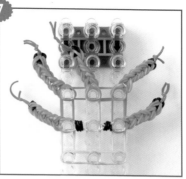

6. You are almost ready to loop your bands back, but first, scoot the bottom red bands to the inside of the outer columns, as shown. Now loop your bands back to the pegs where they started, beginning at the bottom of the loom. Once finished, carefully remove from the loom and set aside.

7. Lay out green and yellow bands for her face. Wrap two single black bands onto a hook and slide them onto a single yellow band that has been wrapped on itself. These will be the eyes; attach them to the middle of her face. Create six snakes for her hair by knitting chains made first of a black single band, followed by green double bands. Add knotted single red bands to the heads of the snakes, and

snip the ends to look like their tongues. Attach these six snakes to her hair on the loom.

8. Attach Medusa's body to the bottom of her head. Starting from the bottom of her head, loop the bands back to the pegs where they started. Secure with an extra rubber band or a c-clip when you finish, and carefully remove from the loom.

MERMAN

Check out what's under the sea! This cool merman is twenty
thousand leagues of fun and is super simple to make. Once you have
him made, make sure to pair him with your other sea creatures!

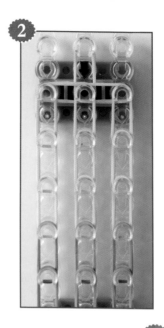

Set up your loom square so the three columns are all in an even line. All the bands will be double bands unless otherwise mentioned.

1. Begin by laying out the torso of the merman, as shown.

2. Change colors to start his fins, going all the way down the loom until you have done six rows. Close off the fin by bringing the bands to a point.

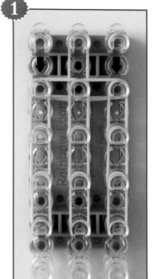

3. Lay out crossover bands to secure the body. These are single bands that are wrapped once on themselves before they are placed across the figure. You will have a total of eight crossover bands.

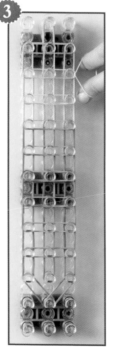

4. Create the split in the fins by wrapping a single band around your hook. Slide this onto a double band.

5. Repeat this until you have a whole fin. Make two fins total.

6. Attach both fins to the bottom center peg in the figure.

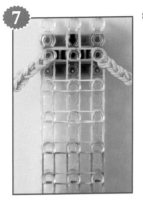

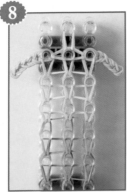

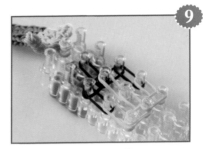

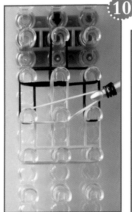

7. Create the arms in the same way you created the fins, but add an extra stitch or two. Place them at the top of the figure.

8. Loop the bands back to the pegs where they came from, starting with the fins at the bottom.

9. Set the body aside and create the face of the merman, as shown.

10. Wrap a band that is the same color as the merman's face on itself so that it is taut. Wrap two separate black bands onto a hook. Slide both of these bands onto the tight band, and attach it to the center of the merman's face.

11. Attach the body of the merman to the bottom of his face. Starting from this peg, loop the project back to the top of his head and secure before removing from the loom.

BUTTERFLY

Turn those rubber band caterpillars into beautiful butterflies! This super cute project has a few moving parts, but it is very easy to assemble. Try making many of them in all sorts of colors for a kaleidoscope of butterflies!

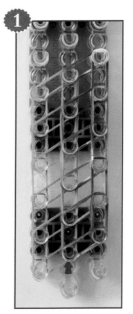

Set up your loom so that the center column is offset, with one peg closer to you and the arrow facing away. All bands are double bands unless otherwise mentioned.

1. For the first large wing, start from the left column and move right. Lay out a line of pink double bands, then rows of pink double bands to connect to the center column. Lay out a line of pink double bands in the center column, and then rows of purple double bands to connect to the right-hand column. Finally, lay out a line of purple double bands, securing the top peg with a white cap band.

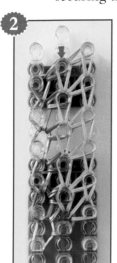
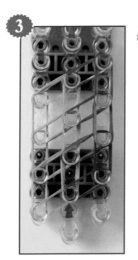

2. Turn the loom around and loop the bands back to the pegs where they started, beginning from the white cap band. Secure the top of the wing with a purple band and c-clip before removing from the loom and setting aside. The c-clips are temporary. Repeat these steps for the second large wing.

3. For the smaller wings, you will repeat the same process but with fewer bands.

4. Turn the loom around and begin from the white cap band as you loop

the project back. Secure with a purple band and c-clip, remove from the loom, and repeat for the second small wing.

5. Set the wings aside and make the head of the butterfly using white double bands.

6. Lay out white double bands down the entire center column to create the body of the butterfly, ending with a cap band.

7. Attach crossover bands to the head as well as the eyes using a white band that has been threaded through two black knots.

8. Make two antennae by creating a chain of pink and purple double bands. Attach these and the wings to the loom, as shown. (Remove the c-clips before attaching the wings.)

9. Loop the project back, starting from the bottom of the body. Be careful while looping the areas where the wings connect—it can be tricky! Secure the top of the project with a c-clip before removing from the loom.

ALiEN

This little green alien comes together faster than you can say "out of this world"! Make a bunch and start your own invasion!

Difficulty level: **Easy**

You need:

1 loom • 1 hook • green and black bands

1. Starting at the first middle peg, use double bands to lay a long hexagon shape onto the loom. Lay out the left side, then the right side.

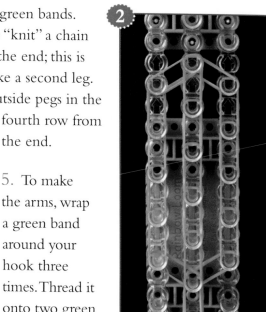

2. Lay a line of double bands up the center column, ending on the sixth peg. Using green double bands, lay a long hexagon shape onto the loom for the body. Lay out the left side, then the right side. Lay a line of double green bands down the middle of the body shape.

3. Wrap a green band around your hook three times. Use your hook to "knit" a chain two loops long with the green band on the end. Repeat to make another chain.

4. Thread both chains onto two green bands. Continue to use your hook to "knit" a chain five loops long with a fork at the end; this is your alien's leg. Repeat to make a second leg. Place the legs onto the two outside pegs in the

fourth row from the end.

5. To make the arms, wrap a green band around your hook three times. Thread it onto two green bands. Continue to "knit" with

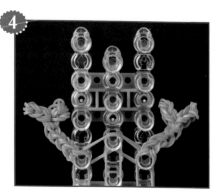

your hook until you have a chain about *eight* loops long with the wrapped band at the end. Repeat to make another chain the same length. Attach your arms to your alien's body shape.

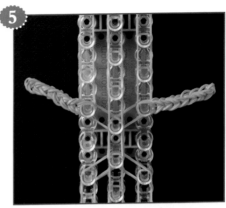

6. Wrap two separate black bands onto your hook. Thread them onto a single green band and attach it to the second row in a triangle shape. Make sure the eyes are pushed to each side.

7. Wrap a green band around your hook twice, then attach it to the third row on the loom in a triangle shape. Continue laying out triangle shapes down your alien's body, using single bands doubled over. You'll lay out six triangles total. Wrap a cap band around the last middle peg three times.

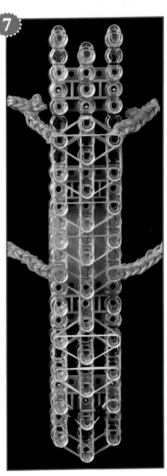

8. Starting at the last middle peg, loop your bands back where they started. Tie off the last loops with a single green band or use a c-clip.

PeNGUiN

Hit the Antarctic with this waddling loom friend! This fun penguin will make for a happy addition to your loom zoo creatures and is a cinch to make! So bundle up and get working on this chill conqueror of the South Pole.

Difficulty level: **Easy**

You need:

1 loom • 1 hook • 1 c-clip • blue, black, white, dark orange, and light orange bands

Set up your loom square so that the columns are aligned evenly and the arrows are pointing toward you. All bands are double bands.

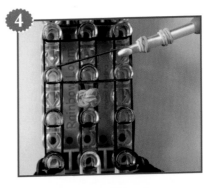

1. Lay out the penguin's head with black double bands, as shown.

2. Lay out a row of light orange double bands, followed by white double bands, as shown.

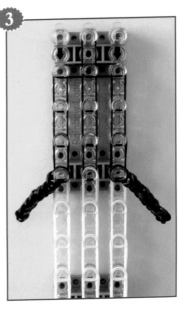

3. Knit two chains of black double bands for each of the arms. Attach to the shoulders of the penguin.

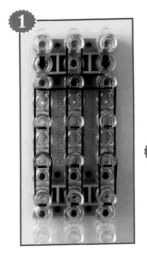

4. Make a beak by knitting a short chain of dark orange double bands (just two knots). Connect to the project using a black band. Add eyes by sliding knotted blue bands from your hook to a black band that has been wrapped once on itself so it is taut.

5. Attach white crossover bands to the body of the penguin. These will be double bands that are stretched across each set of pegs. Add feet by making more short

chains of black double bands and attaching them to the loom.

6. Starting from the feet, loop the bands back to the pegs where they started.

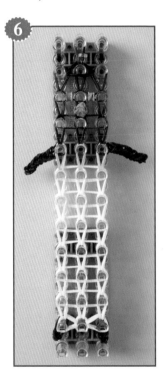

7. Attach a c-clip and gently remove from the loom.

CRAB

Make your day a little sunnier with this beach-dwelling creature, even on a snow day! Pay attention to the color changes to make a tie-dyed shell that's extra cool!

Difficulty level: **Easy**

You need:

1 loom • 1 hook • white, light orange, dark orange, and black bands

1. Lay a line of white double bands down the left and center columns, ending on the fourth peg.

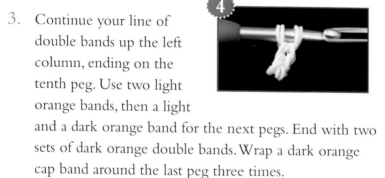

2. Continue your line of double bands, using a white and a light orange band to connect the fifth and sixth pegs. Use light orange double bands to connect the sixth and seventh pegs on the left and for the diagonal band from the center peg to the left.

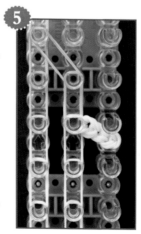

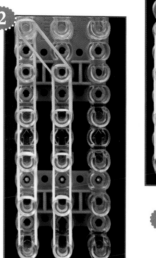

3. Continue your line of double bands up the left column, ending on the tenth peg. Use two light orange bands, then a light and a dark orange band for the next pegs. End with two sets of dark orange double bands. Wrap a dark orange cap band around the last peg three times.

4. Wrap a white band onto your hook three times. Thread it onto two white bands. Use your hook to continue "knitting" a chain four loops long. Use a white and a light orange band for your last pair of bands.

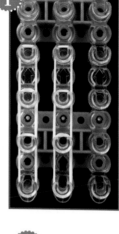

5. Place your chain onto the loom on the middle peg right above the fork.

6. Wrap a white band around your hook twice, and place it over the left and middle pegs in

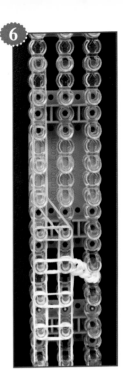

6

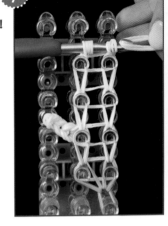

7

the fourth row. Repeat for the third and second row.

7. Turn your loom and begin looping your bands back to where they started. Put your hook through the last two loose loops and remove your crab's claw from the loom. Repeat steps 1 through 7 to make a second claw.

9

8. Attach two dark orange bands to the first middle peg, and connect it to the next middle peg. Starting on the second middle peg, lay out a long hexagon of dark orange double bands. Lay a line of dark orange double bands down the middle of your hexagon shape.

10

9. To make the legs, wrap a dark orange band onto your hook three times. Thread it onto two dark orange bands. Use your hook to "knit" a chain five loops long (not counting the first tripled band). Use dark orange for the first three loops, then use a light and a dark orange and use two light orange bands for the last loop.

10. Repeat to make six total legs. Attach your legs and your claw from earlier to the loom, as shown.

11. Wrap two separate black bands around your hook three times. Thread them onto a single dark orange band, and place the band onto the third row on your loom in a triangle shape. Make sure the black bands are pushed to the outside.

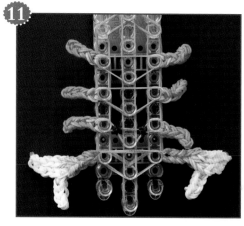

12. Turn your loom around and begin looping your bands back where they started. Secure the last two loose loops with a c-clip and remove your crab from the loom.

GiNGERBREAD MAN

Yum! This gingerbread man is cute enough to eat! But you probably shouldn't, because he is made of rubber bands.

Difficulty level: **Medium**

You need:

1 loom • 1 hook • brown bands • 2 black bands • 2 green bands • 4 white bands

Set up your loom square with the arrow facing away from you.

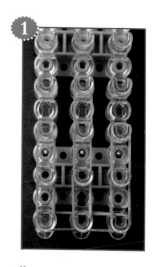

1. Lay double bands across the first row, moving from left to right. Lay a line of double bands up each column.

2. Attach double bands to the third peg on the left, and connect it to the next middle peg. Do the same on the right. Lay double bands across the fourth row, moving from left to right.

3. Attach two bands to the center peg in the fourth row, and connect it to the next middle peg. Lay a line of double bands down the outside columns, ending on the tenth peg.

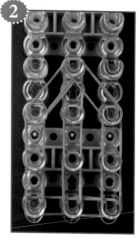

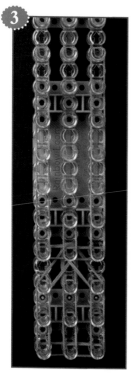

4. Wrap a green band around your hook three times, and thread it onto double brown bands. Lay it onto the loom above your last middle band. Repeat to make a second button, and place it above the first one, as shown.

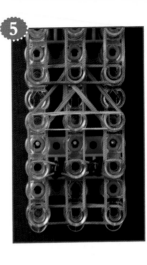

5. Wrap two separate black bands onto your hook three times and thread them onto two brown bands. Attach it to the second row on your loom.

6. Lay two pairs of double bands down the outside columns of your loom at the bottom of your gingerbread body shape. Wrap a cap band around each of the last pegs three times.

7. Use the bottom of your loom to make the arms: lay down two lines of double bands, as shown, and wrap a cap band around the last peg in each line three times. Loop your arm bands as usual.

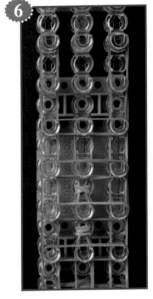

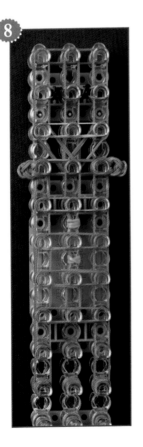

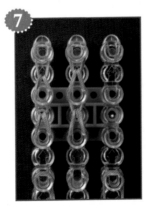

8. Remove the arms from the loom, and stack the loose loops onto the outside pegs in the fourth row.

9. Turn your loom around, and loop the outside columns of your gingerbread man all the way up to his neck. Pull the horizontal band between his legs so that it is not on the center peg.

10. Loop the middle column, then loop the head shape normally.

11. Remove your gingerbread man from the loom. Wrap a white band around your hook twice, then slide it around his ankle. Do this with the rest of his limbs.

STARFiSH

Hit the beach with this awesome starfish! Mix your colors to form one of the coolest underwater creatures in seas near and far. This project is super easy, and you can create a whole kingdom of them to decorate your room or bring swimming with you!

Difficulty level: **Easy**

You need:

1 loom • 1 hook • 2 colors of bands

Set up the loom so the center column is offset one peg away from you. All the bands will be double bands made of two different colors.

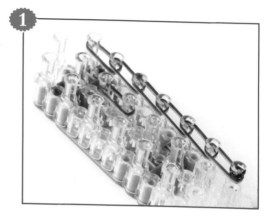

1. Lay out a series of six double bands in the far right column and one double band partway down the center column, as shown. Wrap a cap band on the bottom peg in the right column.

2. Starting from the bottom peg with the cap band, begin to loop the bands back to the pegs where they started. When you reach the peg near the center bands, loop diagonally across to the center bands.

3. Return to the right column and loop once more, then carry the looped bands from the center column over to this peg, as shown.

4. Carefully remove this from the loom and set aside. Create a total of five starfish arms.

5. Place the starfish arms on the loom, using the loops to spread between pegs.

6. Continue in a circular fashion around the loom. There will be one area that will not have an arm. Make a figure eight with a double band and attach to this area to connect the sides of the starfish.

7. Starting from the "two o'clock" peg, lay out six double bands from the center peg around the circle. The double bands should be the same color.

8. From the bands that you laid down last, loop these bands back, as shown.

9. Next, loop the bands going around the circumference of the starfish. Secure a band at the top of the project and carefully remove from the loom.

LOOM
Magic Charms!

Designs by Neary Alguard

T-Rex

For the fiercest of loom projects, meet the T-Rex! This Tyrannosaurus looks just like the real thing, but luckily for you, we are not in the Cretaceous Period and he is not made of sharp claws and teeth. This project has a lot of steps for his many different body parts, so just be careful to follow all of the steps in order.

Difficulty level: **Hard**

You need:

1 loom • 2 hooks • dark green bands • red bands • white bands • black bands

Set up your loom offset so that the center column is one peg farther from you.

1. First you will make the T-Rex's mouth. For the top jaw, lay out the figure shown using green double bands. Attach a cap band at the bottom center peg.

2. Using single bands that have been "doubled," or wrapped once on themselves, lay out two triangular holding bands. To make his nostrils, wrap two separate single bands around your hook several times. Slide both of them onto another single green band and attach this to your loom at the fourth outside pegs.

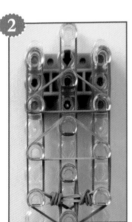

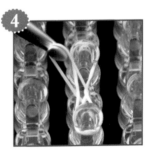

3. For the teeth, you will attach a single band to the loom, wrapping it in a figure eight.

4. Using your hook, take the bottom band on one side and loop it over the peg to the center of the band. Do this again on the opposite side.

5. Your teeth should look like little knots. Repeat this process eleven more times for a total of twelve teeth.

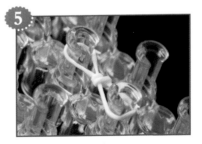

6. Attach the teeth to the second, third, and fourth pegs on the left and right sides of the figure. Starting from the

cap band at the bottom, loop the jaw back to the top of the loom. Before removing from the loom, secure the top three bands temporarily on a holding hook or with c-clips. Set aside.

7. For the bottom part of the jaw, attach green double bands to your loom in the figure shown. Note that the diagonal bands have been attached after the band between pegs 1 and 2 in the outside columns, but before the outside bands from pegs 2 to 3. Fill in the center column last and finish with a cap band.

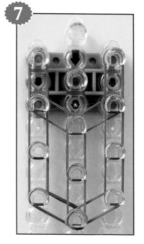

8. Attach three single holding bands to the project. These bands will be "doubled," meaning that they have been wrapped once on themselves so they are tight. Add the remaining teeth to the second, third, and fourth pegs in the left and right columns.

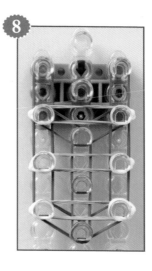

9. Starting from the cap band, carefully loop the bands back to the pegs where they started. Like the top part of the jaw, secure the top of the project with a holding hook or c-clips, remove from the loom, and set aside.

10. For the legs, attach green double bands to the loom for seven rows. Note the fifth and sixth bands have been "doubled" to make them tight. Attach a cap band to the bottom peg. Add two bands just before the top of the center column—this will help make the thigh look bigger.

11. Before looping the legs back, you will need to make the T-Rex's claws by creating tiny single chains. Wrap a white band around your hook several times.

12. Slide the white band onto a green band that has been "doubled" or wrapped once on itself to make it tight. Add two more of these green bands until you have small claws.

13. You will need to create three claws for each foot and arm, for a total of twelve claws.

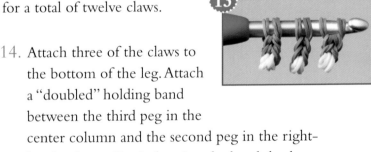

14. Attach three of the claws to the bottom of the leg. Attach a "doubled" holding band between the third peg in the center column and the second peg in the right-hand column. Begin looping the bands back to the pegs where they started. After you've reached the fourth peg from the top, loop the band diagonally to the bands in the center column. Finish looping the center column, and then return to finish looping the right-hand column. Secure both of these top loops with a holding hook or a c-clip and set aside. Make two legs.

15. For the T-Rex's short arms, create a single chain using three bands. The first band will be a double band, and the second two will be single bands that have been "doubled" so they are tight. Attach the three claws to the bottom peg and add a cap band.

16. Starting from the cap band, loop the bands in the arm back to where they started. Secure the arm on a holding hook or with a c-clip and set aside. Make two arms total.

17. For the tail, lay out the figure shown using green single bands on the outside columns and double bands on the inside column. Attach the bands in the center column first, followed by the outside columns. Note that the diagonal bands stretch an extra peg-length. Finish the end of the tail with a cap band.

18. Add five triangular holding bands that have been "doubled" and one regular holding band at the bottom of the tail, which will also be "doubled."

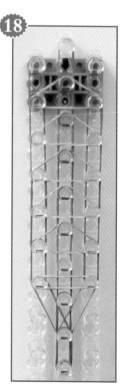

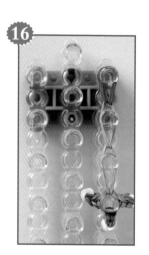

19. Starting from the cap band at the bottom, loop the bands in your project back to the pegs where they started. Secure the tops of the project and set aside.

20. For the T-Rex's head, lay out the small hexagon shown using single bands. Fill in the center column after you have laid out the hexagon.

21. Thicken the neck by attaching a double band between the second and third pegs in the center column. Continue the figure in the arrangement shown—make sure to add the double band in the center column after the first set of diagonal bands but before the second set of diagonal bands.

22. Finish the torso by making a large hexagon. The outside columns will be single bands and the center column will be double bands.

23. For the eyes, wrap a black band around your hook several times. Slide it onto a "doubled" red band. Once you have two eyes, slide these onto a single green band. Attach the eyes across the second outside pegs, then attach a single triangular holding band. Lay out three more triangular holding bands across the torso.

24. Carefully attach the tail, legs, and arms to the T-Rex's body. Note that the arms attach to the diagonal shoulder bands—so you will wait to add

them until you reach the shoulder bands in your looping process. Loop all of the bands up to the face, then stop just before the top so you can add the mouth.

25. Attach the bottom part of the jaw to the second outside pegs.

26. Attach the top part of the jaw to the same row, though this time you will be attaching the three bands over each peg in the row. This part will have a lot of bands, so you may find it easiest to loop the face bands as you attach each part of the top jaw to secure it. Once the jaws are secure, finish looping the rest of the project and secure the head at the top before removing the project from the loom.

27. Once the T-Rex is off the loom, you may need to fiddle with the bands to get his eyes out front or to make him sit the way you like.

TOP HAT

Fancy up your loom charms with this great top hat! Use it as a charm to dangle from a keychain, or put it on top of your favorite loom animals! This project is quick and easy and makes a great accessory!

Difficulty level: **Easy**

You need:

1 loom • 1 hook • 1 or 2 c-clips (optional) • black bands •
7 color bands

Set up your loom square. All bands will be double bands.

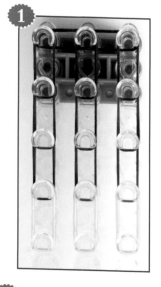

1. Lay out the figure of black and gold double bands, as shown.

2. Attach single black holding bands over the second and third rows, and then attach a single gold holding band over the third row. Attach black cap bands to each of the three bottom pegs.

3. Loop the bands back to the pegs where they started, doing the outside columns first. Loop the horizontal bands in the

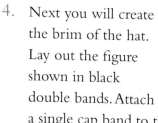

first row to the center, then loop the middle column. Attach a c-clip or a band to the top of the project. Remove the hat from the loom and set aside.

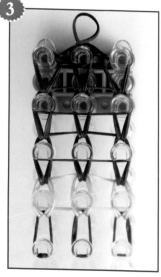

4. Next you will create the brim of the hat. Lay out the figure shown in black double bands. Attach a single cap band to the corner of the project where you placed the last set of bands.

5. Take the top of the hat and put it upside down into the gap in the loom. Attach each of the black loops in the hat to the corresponding

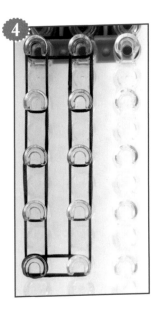

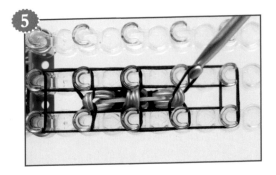

middle pegs (each loop should attach to two pegs).

6. Starting with the cap band in the brim and moving to the peg in the opposite column, loop the bands back to the pegs where they started. Loop the two columns going from bottom to top (do not loop in a square).

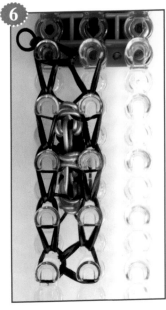

7. Attach a single band or a c-clip to tie off the project. Gently remove from the loom.

SUNFLOWER

This sunny flower will brighten your day! This project is simple to put together, but because the bands are tight, it does take a little extra concentration to make sure they don't snap. If you would like to make a bigger flower, simply replace the single bands with double bands throughout the project.

Difficulty level: **Medium**

You need:

1 loom • 2 hooks • green bands • black bands • yellow bands

Set up your loom offset so that the center column is one peg farther away from you. All bands are single bands that have been "doubled," or wrapped once on themselves.

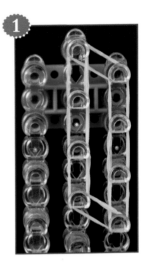

1. For the sunflower petals, lay out the trapezoid in the photo using single bands that have been doubled.

2. Attach two triangle holding bands, as shown. Both of these will be single bands that have been "doubled." Attach a cap band to the bottom right-hand corner of the figure.

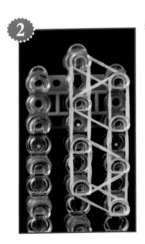

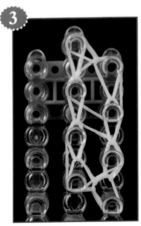

3. Starting from the cap band, loop the left side of the petal up to the top peg. Return to the cap band and loop the right side of the petal, finishing at the top of the loom. Secure the top of the project on a holding hook or with a c-clip.

4. Repeat this five more times for a total of six petals, and set them aside for later.

5. For the leaf that will go on the stem, lay out a slightly smaller version of

the petals you just made. Similarly, these green bands will all be single bands that have been "doubled."

6. Attach a triangular holding band to the petal. This will be a single band that has been "doubled." Add a cap band to the bottom peg on the right-hand side of the project.

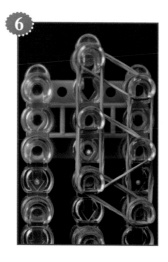

7. Starting from the cap band, loop the left side of the project back up to the top of the loom. Return to the cap band and loop the remaining pegs on the right side of the loom, finishing at the top peg. Secure the leaf and set it aside for later.

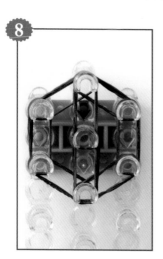

8. For the eye of the sunflower, lay out a hexagon shape using black single bands that have been "doubled." Attach the ones in the center after you have laid out the hexagon.

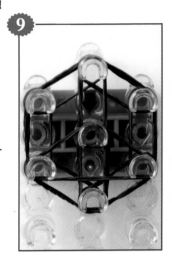

9. Using a single black band that has been "doubled," attach a triangular holding band to the center of the hexagon.

10. Lay out the stem of the flower using green single bands that have been "doubled," as shown. Attach a cap band to the last peg in the stem.

11. Carefully attach the green leaf to the stem, as well as five of the six sunflower petals. Leave the center peg at the bottom of the flower free for the moment.

12. Starting with the cap band, loop the bands back to the pegs where they started, finishing at the top of the stem that connects to the flower.

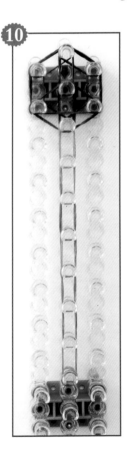

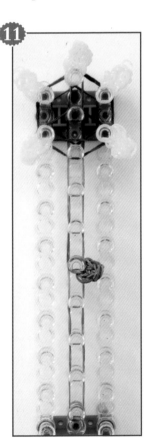

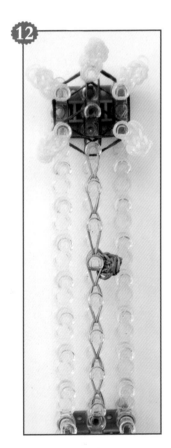

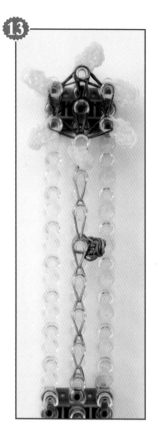

13 Attach the remaining petal to the center bottom peg in the flower (just at the top of the stem). Loop the black bands back to the pegs where they started. Since there are so many bands, it may be helpful to use another hook to release the tension as you go.

14 Secure the project and gently remove from the loom.

FLiP FLOPS

Get ready for beach weather with these cool sandals! This super easy project is great for jewelry—just attach the top of the flip flops to earring hooks or to a funky bracelet.

Difficulty level: **Easy**

You need:

1 loom • 1 hook • purple bands • white bands

Set up your loom offset, so that the center column is one peg away from you. All bands will be single bands that have been "doubled," or wrapped once on themselves so they are taut.

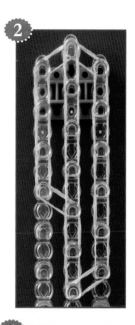

1. Lay out the beginning of your flip flop in the formation shown. Make sure you are using single bands that have been "doubled."

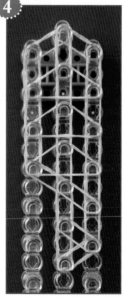

2. Add to the formation by attaching six more bands down the center column. Connect this column to the right-hand side with a diagonal band.

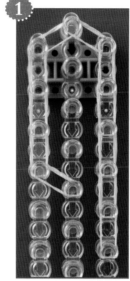

3. Lay out five holding bands: three triangle-shaped and two smaller ones. All of these should be single bands that have been "doubled." Attach a cap band to the bottom of the project.

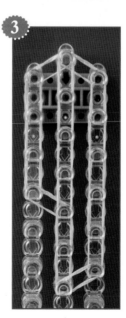

4. Loop the bands back to the pegs where they started. Make sure to start with the bands closest to the top of the pegs. Loop the center column only part way.

5. Finish looping the rest of the center column. Doing this last will help hold the project together.

6. Take two single white bands and wrap them in slipknots at either side of the flip flops.

7. For added effect, twist the white bands several times before securing them at the top of the sandal with another rubber band.

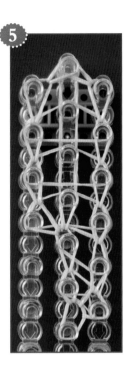

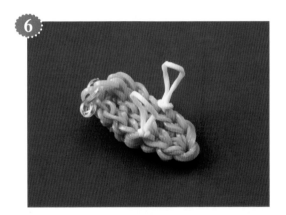

DOLLAR SiGN

Money isn't everything, but this rubber band dollar sign hits the jackpot. This project is fun and simple, but just be careful to follow the layout and looping instructions in the correct order.

Difficulty level: **Medium**

You need:

1 loom • 1 hook • rubber bands

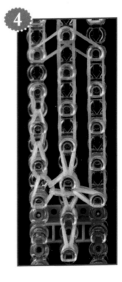

Set up your loom offset so that the center column is one peg farther away from you than the others. All the bands are double bands (two rubber bands used as one).

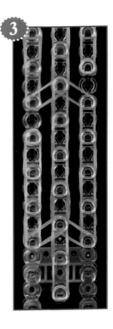

1. Lay out the first figure shown using double bands. Start by adding the first two double bands in the center column. Next, branch out to the outside columns, laying the bands from the top down. Add the center column, and then connect the center column to the left column with a double band.

2. Continue down the dollar sign, forming the center column and the bottom right side of the "S."

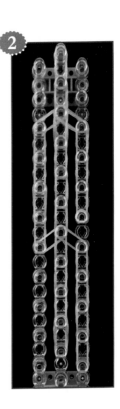

3. Lay out the rest of the "S," making sure to move clockwise as if you were writing the "S" with a pen. Add the bottom two double bands to finish the center column. Attach cap bands to both ends of the "S," as well as at the bottom of the dollar sign.

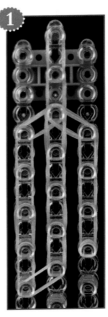

4. Starting with the cap band at the tail of the dollar sign, loop the first two bands back to the pegs where they started. Then go to the end of the S, and begin looping back those bands. This part of the "S" will feel funny to loop because bands are not ordinarily laid out from bottom to top, but this is okay. When looping the band that connects the center column to the right column, make sure you are moving counterclockwise.

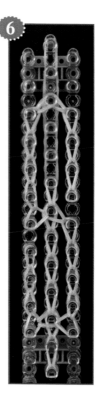

5. Continue looping the bands up to the center of the dollar sign, looping the right-hand column second.

6. Continue clockwise up the rest of the left side of the "S" to the center column. Then, starting from the cap band at the tip of the "S" on the right-hand side, loop the bands back up to the center column.

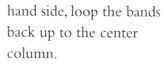

7. Finish looping the center column all the way up to the top of the dollar sign. Tie off the top of the project with a c-clip or an additional single band. Gently remove from the loom.

APPLE

The stem and leaf of this project are both made using all doubled bands, meaning they are extra tight. When looping, you'll want to be careful so you don't break any bands or your hook!

Difficulty level: **Medium**

You need:

1 loom • 1 hook (use a metal hook if you have one) • red bands • green bands • brown bands

1. Wrap a single brown band around your hook twice, then attach it from the second to the third peg in the left column. Repeat to continue laying out the stem as shown using tight doubled bands.

2. Lay out your apple's leaf shape using tight doubled bands. Start at the fourth middle peg and lay out two sets of green single bands, doubled, down the middle column, then attach another doubled green band from the first peg on the right to the second middle peg. Go back to the fourth middle peg and lay out the right half of the leaf shape, ending on the first peg on the right.

3. Place two doubled green bands across your leaf shape as holding bands. Wrap a single green band three or four times around the first peg on the right as a cap band.

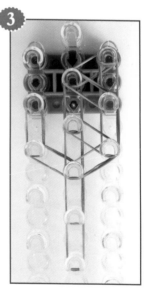

4. Using double red bands, lay out your apple shape. Lay out the left side, starting at the sixth and ending on the ninth middle peg, then lay out the right side.

5. Take two red bands and wrap them around your hook twice, then attach them from the sixth to the seventh middle peg. Repeat twice more down the middle of your apple shape.

6. Attach holding bands to your apple shape. Take two red bands and attach them to the center of the apple in a triangle shape. Attach a single band across the row above the triangle and another across the row below. Wrap a single red band around the bottom middle peg of your apple three or four times as a cap band.

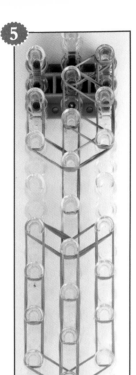

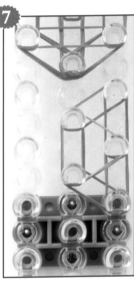

7. Using single bands, lay out a trapezoid shape below your apple. Layout the left side, then the right side. Wrap a single band around the last peg in the right column as a cap band. Wrap a single red band around your hook twice and attach it to the trapezoid in a triangle shape as a holding band.

8. Loop your extra piece, looping each side out from the cap band and ending on the peg where you started.

9. Remove your extra piece from the loom and attach it to the side of your apple shape, placing the loose loops onto the top corner peg and the cap band end onto the third peg down. Make the other extra piece in the same way, and attach it to the other side of the apple.

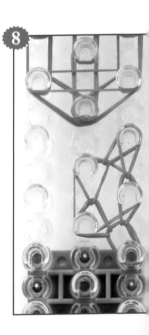

10. Begin looping your apple shape: Start at the cap band and loop up the four pegs in the middle column. Then loop the outside columns to the same last peg. When you have looped all the red bands, loop the first doubled brown band. Loop the leaf

shape next; you will be looping backwards for some of the bands. Loop the peg with the cap band, then loop out in both directions to end on the fourth middle peg where it attaches to the stem.

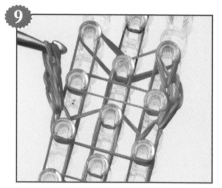

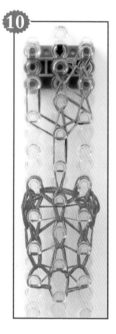

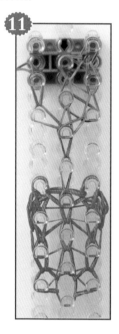

11. Finish looping your stem, working your way up until you have looped all the bands on your loom. Secure the final loose bands with a single brown band pulled in a slip knot.

12. Remove your apple from the loom.

TREBLE CLEF

Make beautiful music with this multicolored symbol! This is built all with double bands, so it's extra sturdy.

Set up your loom offset with the middle column pulled away from you one peg.

1. Lay a line of double bands down the left column, then lay a line of double bands halfway down the right column. If you are making your treble clef rainbow-colored, match the colors in the example, laying out orange, then yellow, then green, then blue bands on the right, and green then yellow bands on the left. Wrap a green band around the last peg in the right column three or four times as a cap band.

2. Loop the bands in your right column.

3. Remove the bands from the right column, and carefully place the loose loops from the end onto the last peg in the left column.

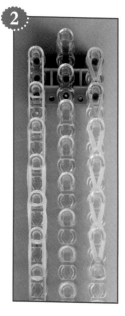

4. Loop your left column, treating the chain you just added as a cap band. Remove your long chain from the loom and set aside for now.

5. Using purple bands, lay a line of double bands down the left

column, ending on the sixth peg. Wrap a blue band around the sixth peg three or four times as a cap band.

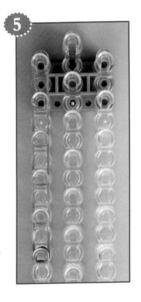

6. Loop your row as usual. Remove your chain from the loom and set aside.

7. Using double bands, lay a line of red bands down the middle column from the first to the fourth peg. Starting at the first and ending on the fourth middle peg, lay out a trapezoid shape to the right using red and orange bands. Then lay a line of bands down the middle column, starting at the fourth middle peg and continuing to the end of the loom. Follow the color changes of the example if you are making your treble clef rainbow-colored.

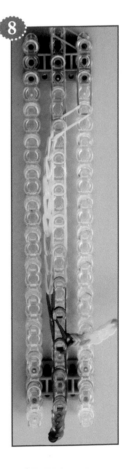

8. Attach the chains you had set aside. Place the purple chain onto the last middle peg. For

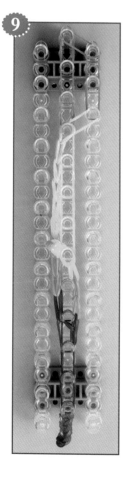

the longer chain, attach the orange end to the fourth middle peg, then find the eleventh stitch in the chain (counting the orange stitch), and loop it onto the third peg from the end.

9. Find the third stitch from the end of your same long chain, and attach it to the sixth peg from the end. Make sure you are laying the added chain parts down as shown so that your treble clef is shaped correctly.

10. Loop your treble clef shape as usual. Secure the last loops with a red single band pulled into a slipknot; do not pull the knot too tight or it will mess up your treble clef shape.

BANANA

This may just be the easiest charm there is! With just a few rubber bands and a simple banana shape, this light snack will be at your loom monkey's side in no time!

Difficulty level: **Easy**

You need:

1 loom • 1 hook • yellow bands • 2 brown or green bands

Set up your loom offset so the center column is one peg further away from you.

1. Lay out the banana shape shown, using single yellow bands that have been "doubled," or that have been wrapped once on themselves.

2. Add a brown cap band to the bottom right corner of the banana.

3. Using more single bands that have been "doubled," lay out holding bands to make the project tight. Notice that the holding bands in the top left corner look like a triangle.

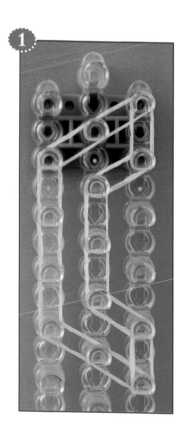
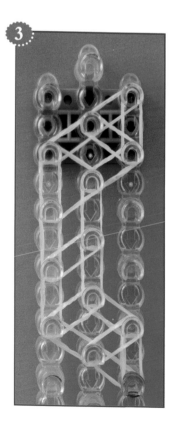

4. Starting from the brown cap band, loop the bands back to the pegs where they started. Start with one side of the project until you reach the end of the banana, and then go back and do the other side until you reach the end of the banana.

5. Tie off the project with a brown or green rubber band and gently remove from the loom.

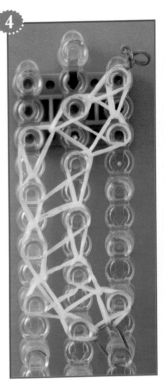

GiRAFFe

Y ou can replace any of your orange bands with brown bands to make spots, like we've done for this example. Make sure to work slowly when looping bands that have been doubled; they are extra tight, so be careful you don't break the bands or your hook!

Difficulty level: **Medium**

You need:

1 loom • 1 hook • orange bands • brown bands • white bands • black bands

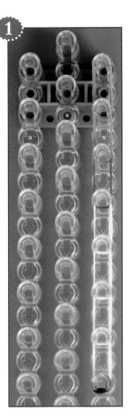

To Make the Legs:

1. Attach three orange bands from the first to the second peg in the right column. Continue laying a line of bands down that column, laying down two sets of double orange bands. Then wrap a white band around your hook twice and attach it from the fourth to the fifth peg. Lay out three more white bands this way. Wrap a black cap band around the last peg (the eighth peg) three times.

2. Starting at the peg where you placed the cap band, loop the bands in your leg. Remove the leg from the loom and set aside. Repeat to make four total legs.

To Make the Horns:

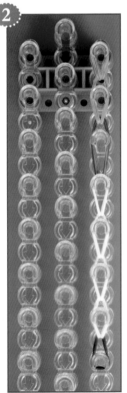

1. Wrap an orange band around your hook twice, then connect it to the first and second pegs in the left column. Repeat and attach the doubled orange band to the second and third pegs. Wrap a white cap band around the third peg three times.

2. Loop your horn as usual. Pull two orange bands through the

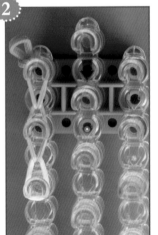

final loose loop to secure it, then remove the horn from your loom, keeping the double orange bands on your hook. Repeat to make your second horn, and leave it on your hook as well.

To Make Your Giraffe:

1. Attach the double orange bands from one of your horn pieces to the first middle and first left pegs. Attach the double bands from the other horn to the first middle and first right pegs.

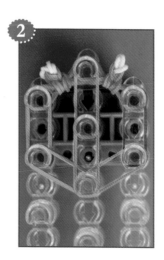

2. Using brown and orange double bands, lay out a small hexagon shape for your giraffe's head, starting where you laid out the giraffe's horns. Lay double orange bands down the middle of the small hexagon shape.

3. Lay out your giraffe's neck. Attach double orange bands from the third to the fourth middle peg. Attach a single orange band to the third middle peg and connect it to the left. Repeat and connect it to the right. Continue to lay double bands down the center and single bands down the outside columns, ending on the ninth peg.

4. Lay out your giraffe's body: attach double orange bands to the ninth middle peg, and connect them to the left. Repeat and connect to the right. Lay double

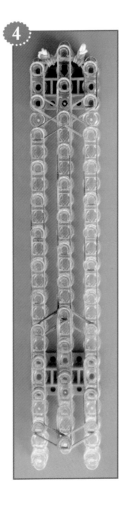

bands down the center column to the end and down the outside columns to the second to last peg. Close off your body shape by connecting double bands from the second to last outside pegs to the last middle peg. Wrap a cap band around the last middle peg three or four times.

5. Attach your giraffe's legs. Connect the front legs to the outside columns five pegs from the end. Attach the back legs to the outside columns two pegs from the end.

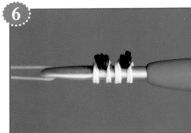

6. Make your giraffe's eyes. Wrap a black band around your hook four times. Double a white band onto itself and thread the black band onto the doubled white band. Put both ends of the white band onto the hook. Leaving your first eye on the hook, repeat to make the second. Stretch a single orange band between the hook and your finger and thread the eyes onto this. Leave it on your hook or set it aside for now.

7. Make your giraffe's ears. Wrap an orange band around your hook four times, then stretch double orange bands between your hook and your fingers

and thread the wrapped band onto it.
Repeat to make the second ear.

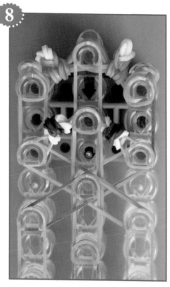

8. Attach your eyes and ears, as shown. Pull
the middle of the "eye" band over the
second middle peg, making sure to push
the eyes to either side.

9. Lay "holding bands" across the whole
shape. Wrap a single orange band around
your hook twice and stretch it across the
second row in a triangle shape. Repeat to
lay triangle shapes down the whole body
shape, as shown. In the eighth row, pull the
holding band into a diamond shape. Wrap
a single orange band around your hook twice

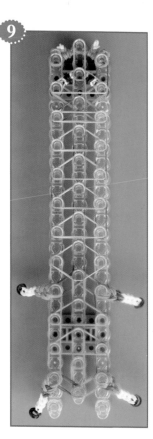

and place the band across the
third row. Place single bands in
triangle shapes across the two
rows between your giraffe's legs;
do not double them.

10. Starting at the peg where
you placed your cap band,
begin looping your giraffe
shape. Loop as usual all
the way up to the "chin"
peg (the third middle peg).
Once you have looped
the chin peg, you will add
additional bands for the
giraffe's snout.

11. Push the bands of your giraffe's head down the pegs. Attach double white bands from the second to the third and the third to the

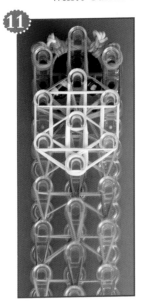

fourth middle pegs. Wrap a white band around your hook and attach it from the second to the third peg on the right. Repeat on the left. Place a doubled white band from the third outside peg to the fourth middle peg on either side to close your snout shape. Add holding bands by wrapping a band around your hook twice and attaching it to the third row in a triangle shape. Wrap a white band around your hook three times, and attach it to the second row (you can loop it twice if three times is too tight). Wrap a white band around the fourth middle peg three times for a cap band.

12. Loop the remaining bands of your giraffe. Pull double orange bands through the final loose loops and tie a slip knot to secure them. Remove your giraffe.

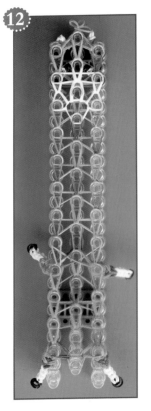

ELEPHANT

This is one pachyderm that won't leave peanuts all over your bedroom! Because you need to attach the ear to your elephant at specific points, the ear is laid out in a strange order; make sure to read the instructions carefully!

Difficulty level: **Easy**

You need:

1 loom • 1 hook • purple bands • light purple bands • pink bands • blue bands • white bands

To Make the Ears:

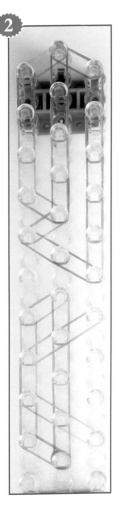

1. Use single purple bands to lay out the ear
   shape. Start at the fifth peg on the right and
   lay a line of single bands up the column,
   ending on the first middle peg. Starting
   at the first middle peg, lay out a trapezoid
   shape in the left column, ending on the fifth
   middle peg. Attach a single band from the
   fifth middle peg to the fifth peg on the left,
   then lay out diagonal bands from there to
   the sixth peg on the right. Lay a single band
   from the sixth to the fifth left peg to close
   the shape.

2. Lay out single bands in a trapezoid shape
   to make the extra piece for your ear. Lay
   out each half starting from the middle peg
   just below your ear shape. Wrap a single
   band around the eleventh middle peg three
   or four times as a cap band. Lay connector
   bands across the shape as shown.

3. Loop the extra piece,
   starting at the cap band and
   looping both sides back to
   the seventh middle peg.

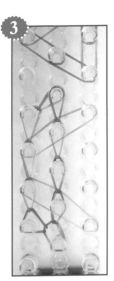

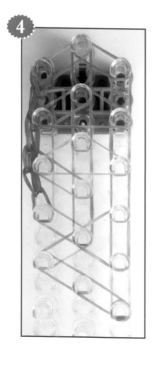

4. Carefully remove the extra piece, holding it by the cap band and by the loose loops from the other end. Place the extra piece onto the left column of the ear, attaching the cap band to the fourth peg, and the loose loops to the first peg. Attach the connector bands to the second and fourth middle pegs. Attach a cap band to the bottom right peg. Attach a single purple holding band to the second row in a triangle shape. Attach a second holding band, doubled, to the third row. Double a single purple band, and attach it to the fourth and fifth right pegs and fifth middle peg in a triangle shape.

5. Starting at your cap band, loop your elephant's ear shape. Loop from the cap band up the right column to the second peg, then stop. From the cap band, loop the three bands going to the left, ending on the middle peg. Loop the rest of the middle column, then go back to the fifth middle peg and loop the left column, working your way around the outside of the ear in a clockwise direction until you reach the second peg in the right column. Secure the loose loops on that second peg, and remove your ear from the loom. Repeat to make your second ear.

To Make the Legs and Trunk:

1. To make your elephant's foot on the hook, wrap two light purple bands around your hook three times, then thread them onto a double purple band. Leave the foot on your hook. For the trunk, wrap a purple and pink band around your hook. Take two purple bands and double them, then thread the pink and purple loops onto the doubled bands.

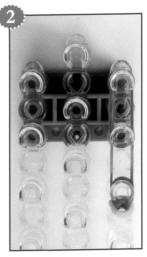

2. Lay a line of double bands down from the first to the third peg. Place your foot onto the third peg as a cap band. For the trunk, wrap your double bands around your hook twice before placing them on the loom, to make them extra tight.

3. Loop your chain back as usual. Carefully remove your leg from the loom and set it aside so that it doesn't unravel. To remove your trunk, pull a single purple band through the loose loops in a temporary slipknot. Make four total legs and one trunk this way.

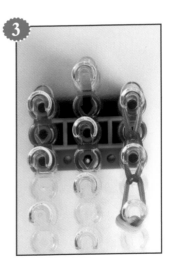

To Make the Body:

1. Using double purple bands, lay out a small hexagon shape onto the loom. Lay double bands down the middle of the shape. Lay out a second small hexagon shape for the elephant's body. Lay double bands down the middle of that hexagon as well.

2. To make the eyes, wrap a blue band around your hook three times, then wrap a single white band around the blue band, wrapping it twice on either side. Repeat to make a second eye on the hook. Thread both eyes onto a single purple band. Place your eyes across the second row, with the middle of the band pulled over the second middle peg.

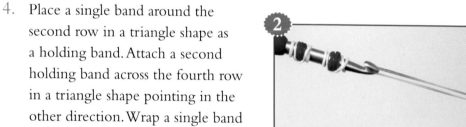

3. Attach your ears by placing the loose loops onto the first outside pegs. Undo the slipknot from your trunk and attach it using the single purple band. Attach your elephant's back legs to the fourth outside pegs.

4. Place a single band around the second row in a triangle shape as a holding band. Attach a second holding band across the fourth row in a triangle shape pointing in the other direction. Wrap a single band around the fifth peg three or four times as a cap band.

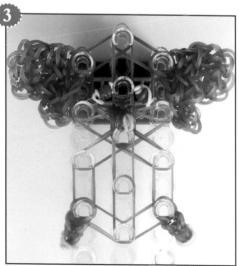

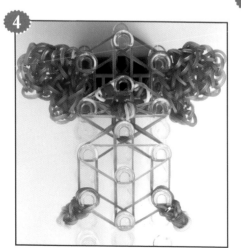

5. Begin looping your elephant, starting at the cap band. Loop the outside columns until you reach the third peg. When you loop from the third outside peg to the third middle (the neck peg), put one of the remaining legs onto your hook, and slide it onto the band before you place it onto the middle peg. Do the same on the other side to attach the other leg.

6. Loop the rest of your elephant shape. Secure the final loose loops with a single band pulled into a slipknot.

7. Remove your elephant from the loom.

FANCY FOX

This fox doesn't say much, but he'll make an excellent (and super cute) addition to your charm collection. Some of the bands in this project are stretched very tightly, so be extra careful when you're looping these.

Difficulty level: **Medium**

You need:

1 loom • 1 hook • orange bands • white bands • black bands • blue (or other eye color) bands

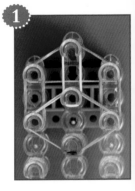

Set up your loom offset, with the middle column pulled one peg up.

To Make the Ears:

1. Lay a single orange band across the first row in a triangle shape. Attach single orange bands from the first to the second peg in each outside column. Wrap an orange band around your hook twice and place it over the third middle peg in a triangle shape. Attach a single white band from the first to the second middle peg. Pull your doubled orange band onto the second middle peg in a diamond shape. Wrap a black cap band around the third middle peg three or four times.

2. Begin looping your ear: grab the top strand of your doubled band. Very slowly, pull the strand up through the cap band and loop it onto the second peg on the right. Pull the other strand to the second left peg in the same way. Loop the outside orange bands and white band as usual. Loop the second orange triangle from the first outside pegs onto the first middle peg. Secure the loose bands and set aside. Make your second ear the same way.

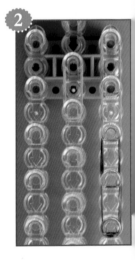

To Make the Legs:

1. Lay out two sets of double orange bands down the right column. Wrap a black band around your hook twice, then stretch it from the third to the fourth peg. Repeat and attach it from the fourth to the fifth peg. Wrap a black cap band around the fifth peg three or four times.

2. For the front legs, loop the bands back as usual. For the back legs, place double orange bands from the second to the third middle peg.

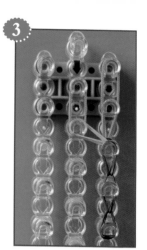

3. For your leg shape, when you loop your orange bands from the third peg, loop them onto the third middle peg. Loop the rest of the bands as usual. Remove the leg from the loom, secure the loose bands with a spare hook, and set aside. Remember to secure both sets of loose loops from the back leg pieces.

To Make the Tail:

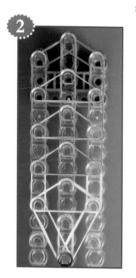

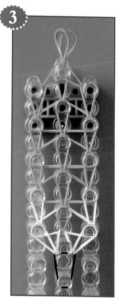

1. Attach a single orange band to the first middle peg and connect it to the right. Repeat and connect it to the left. Lay a line of single orange bands ending in one white band down each column. Wrap a white band around your hook twice and stretch it between the seventh middle peg and the fifth right peg. Repeat on the other side. Wrap a black cap band around the seventh middle peg three or four times.

2. Wrap an orange band around your hook twice, and stretch it onto the second row in a triangle shape. Repeat to make four total triangle shapes across your tail, using a white band for the last triangle.

3. Loop your tail shape as usual, looping the middle column then the outside columns.

4. Secure the loose bands with a spare hook and set aside.

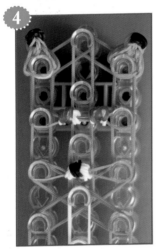

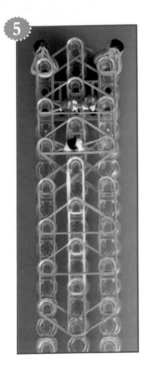

Putting It Together:

1. Use double orange bands to lay out a long hexagon shape for your fox's head. Lay double orange bands down the middle of your hexagon shape. Use double orange bands to lay out a larger hexagon shape for the body. Lay a line of double bands down the middle of the bigger hexagon, starting with white and ending with orange bands.

2. Wrap a black band around your hook four times, then thread it onto two white bands that have been doubled over. This is your snout. Thread the white bands onto a single orange band. Carefully set aside, or place on your spare hook.

3. Wrap a blue band onto your hook four times. Thread it onto a single white band that has been doubled, as you did for the snout. Repeat to make a second eye. Thread both eyes onto a single orange band.

4. Place the single band from your eyes onto the outside pegs in the second row. Place your snout across the third row. Place the ears on the first two pegs on the right and left.

5. Attach a single orange band across the second row in a triangle shape. Repeat in the third row.

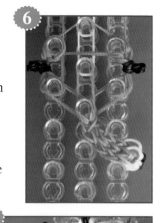

Attach double orange bands to the fifth and sixth rows in a triangle shape.

6. Place the tail onto the eighth middle peg. Attach the back legs to the sixth and seventh pegs in the outside columns.

7. Begin looping your fox shape, starting at the peg where you placed the tail. Loop all the bands from that peg, then continue looping the outside pegs until you reach the diagonal neck pegs.

8. Place one of your front legs onto your hook. Loop the diagonal orange off the fourth outside peg, and thread the loops from your leg onto the band before looping it onto the fourth middle peg. Do the same with the other leg on the other side.

9. Loop the rest of the middle pegs in the body shape. Continue looping your fox as usual.

10. Secure the final loose loops with a single orange band. Remove your fox from the loom. You can tuck the tie-off band into the back of your fox's head using your hook.

OWL

Who? Who else but this adorable owl charm! This project has lots of small parts; some are made on the loom, and some are made with your hook. Make sure to pay attention to the written instructions so you don't miss anything!

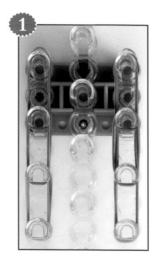

To Make the Wings:

1. Lay a line of double bands down the outside columns, starting on the first and ending on the fourth peg. Use one orange and one gray band per double band. Wrap a single band around the fourth peg on either side three or four times as a cap band.

2. Loop your wings back as usual. Remove from the loom and carefully set aside for now.

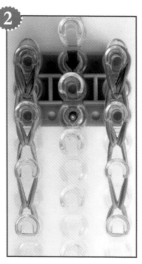

To Make the Body:

1. Using double gray bands, lay out a small hexagon shape onto your loom. Lay a line of double gray bands down the middle of your hexagon.

2. To make the feet, wrap two orange bands around your hook three times, then thread them onto double orange bands. Before looping the end of the double orange bands onto the hook, wrap a single orange band around your hook three times, then loop the end of the double band onto the hook behind it. Thread all the orange bands

onto a double gray band. Set it aside for now, and repeat to make a second foot.

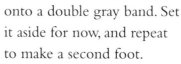

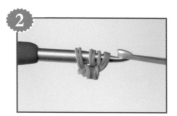

3. Using double gray bands, lay out a longer hexagon shape for your owl's body. For the bottom diagonal bands, place the gray bands from your owl's feet. Lay a line of bands down the middle of your larger hexagon. Use an orange and a gray band for the first double band, then use three gray bands for the next three.

4. To make the eyes, wrap a blue band around your hook four times, then wrap two single white bands around the blue band, twice on either side. Repeat to make the second eye on the hook. Then thread both eyes onto a single gray band. Place across the second row.

5. To make the beak, wrap a single orange band around your hook four times. Then take a double orange band and double it to make it extra tight before threading the single band onto it. Loop both ends of the double orange band onto the hook. Then thread all orange bands onto a single gray band, and place it across the third row.

6. To make the ears, wrap a single gray band around your hook four times. Then thread it onto a doubled gray band. Place the ear onto the first peg on the right, then repeat to make a second and place it on the first peg on the left. Attach your owl's wings to the fourth outside pegs.

7. Place holding bands across your owl shape. Place a single band across the second row in a triangle shape. Repeat across the third, fifth, and sixth rows. Wrap a single band around the last middle peg three or four times as a cap band.

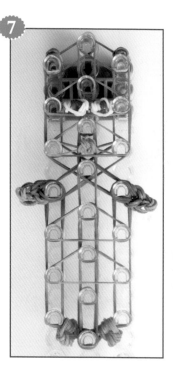

8. Loop your owl shape as usual. Loop the outside pegs up to the neck peg, then loop up the center. Once you have looped the neck peg up to the face, stop. To add extra "poofy cheeks"

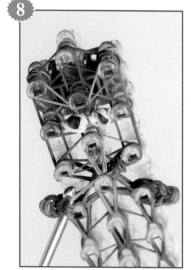

to your owl's face, wrap a single gray band around your hook four times, then pick up the band that is looped back to the third peg on the left, and thread the wrapped gray band onto it before putting it back onto the third left peg. Do the same for the third peg on the right. Attach a single orange band to the first pegs on the right and left, then pull the middle over the second middle peg.

9. Continue looping your owl as usual. Loop the outside pegs of the head shape, then loop the middle pegs. Secure the final loose loops with

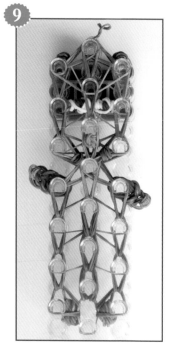

a single gray band pulled into a slipknot. Remove your owl from the loom.

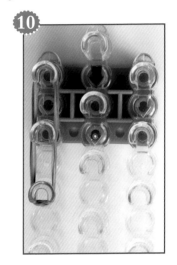

10. To make the tail, wrap three gray bands around your hook twice, then attach them from the first to the second peg. Wrap two gray bands around your hook twice, and attach them from the second to the third peg. Wrap a single gray band around the third peg four or five times as a cap band.

11. Loop your tail back as usual. Thread a single gray band through the final loose loops in a slip knot. Remove the tail from the loom.

12. To attach the tail to your owl, put your hook through a loop in his bottom, then pull the single band from the tail through the loop. Pull the tail through the single gray loop to secure it.

ROCKET

Ready . . . Liftoff! You will "double" some of your bands in this project, so they are extra tight. Many of the other bands in this project are not doubled, though, so make sure to pay attention to the instructions!

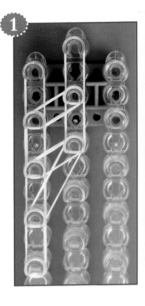

Set up your loom offset, with the middle column pulled one peg up.

To Make the Boosters:

1. Attach a single band from the first to the second peg in the middle and left columns. Continue laying double bands down the left column. Pause on the fourth peg to attach a diagonal double band to the middle column, then continue to the fifth peg. Wrap a cap band around the fifth peg three or four times. Add two doubled bands as holding bands.

2. Loop your booster shape back. Remove and set aside so that it doesn't unravel. Make four total boosters this way.

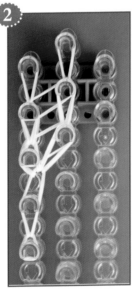

To Make the Fire:

1. Double a single white band, then attach it from the first to the second middle peg. Repeat and attach from the second to the third peg. Wrap a yellow band around your hook and attach it from the second middle to the second left peg. Repeat on the right. Continue laying doubled bands down all three columns, starting with yellow, then switching to orange, and finally red bands. Wrap a single red band around each of the end pegs three or four times as a cap band.

2. Wrap a yellow holding band around your hook twice, then attach it across the second row. Repeat to place a yellow holding band across the third row, then orange across the fourth and fifth rows, and red across the sixth row.

3. Loop your fire, starting from the cap bands and working your way back to the start of the loom. Carefully remove your fire and set it aside.

Make the Rocket Top:

1. Lay out doubled red bands from the first to the fourth peg. Wrap a single red band around the fourth peg three or four times as a cap band.

2. Loop your rocket top back as usual. Carefully remove the piece and set it aside so that it doesn't unravel.

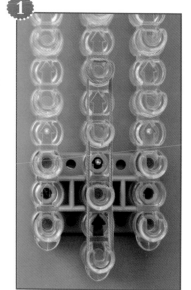

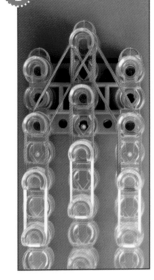

To Make the Rocket Body:

1. Attach two red bands from the first to the second, and another two from the second to the third middle peg. Attach a single red band to the first middle peg and connect it to the second right peg. Repeat on the left side. Attach double red bands from the second to the third outside pegs. Attach double white bands from the third to the fourth peg in all rows.

2. Attach three clear blue jelly bands from the fourth to the fifth and fifth to the sixth middle pegs. Attach three white bands from the sixth to the seventh middle peg, then lay down two more sets of three clear blue jelly bands. Attach three white bands from the ninth to the tenth middle peg. Lay a line of white triple bands up the outside columns, from the fourth to the eighth peg.

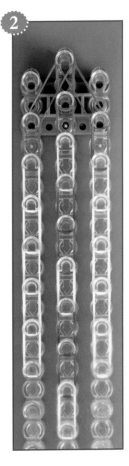

3. Attach three blue jelly bands from the tenth to the eleventh middle peg. Wrap a white band around your hook twice and attach it to the middle column from the eleventh to the twelfth peg. Repeat and place it on the last two pegs in the column. Lay

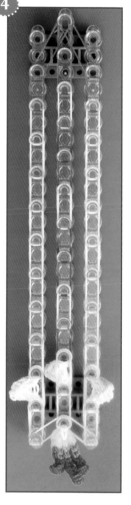

double white bands down the outside columns from the eighth to the second-to-last peg. Attach three white bands from the second-to-last to the last peg in the outside columns. Close up your rocket shape by attaching two white bands from the last middle peg to the last outside peg, then repeat on the other side.

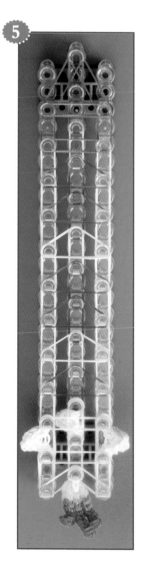

4. Attach your fire to the last middle peg. Attach two of your boosters to the third and second pegs from the end in the outside columns. Attach the third booster to the second and third pegs from the end in the middle column: put the piece point-down and attach the two sets of loops as you did for the other two.

5. Attach holding bands. Wrap a single white band around your hook twice, and attach it across the second-to-last row on the loom. Repeat to attach to the next row. Attach bands in a triangle shape across the rest of the rows of your rocket: use single blue bands for the rows where you have placed windows and double white bands for the non-window rows. Wrap a red band around your hook twice and attach it to the third row. Repeat and attach it to the second row.

6. Attach your last booster piece to the top of the middle column, attaching the two sets of loops to the second and third pegs from the end, with the point facing up.

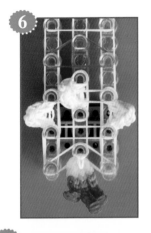

7. Place the rocket top onto the first middle peg.

8. Starting at the last middle peg where you placed your fire piece, begin looping your rocket back. Loop the outside columns, then the middle column. When you reach the booster piece attached to the middle column, make sure to pull the booster piece through the band as you loop it back to the third peg from the end. That way your booster piece will stick out instead of being flattened. Secure the final loose loops with a red single band pulled into a slipknot.

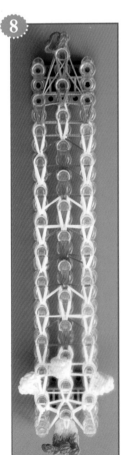

9. Remove your rocket from the loom!

DOLPHiN

Dive into this great project! This fun dolphin makes a delightful friend for your other loom creatures, though we don't promise that he can actually swim.

Difficulty level: **Medium**

You need:

1 loom • 2 hooks • blue bands • white bands

Set up your loom offset so that the center column is one peg farther away from you.

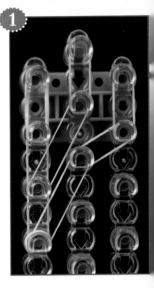

1. Using blue single bands, make the flippers by laying out the figure shown. Note that two of the diagonal bands are stretching the length of two pegs. Attach a cap band to the bottom peg.

2. Attach a triangular holding band across the middle of the fin and a smaller holding band from the third left peg diagonally to the bottom center peg. Both bands are a single band that has been "doubled," or wrapped once on itself.

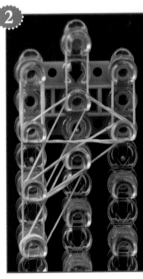

3. Starting from the cap band, loop the bands back to the pegs where they started. Make sure to loop the diagonal bands, but not the holding bands.

4. To make the dorsal fin, you will use a slightly smaller layout than the flippers. Create the shape shown using single blue bands. Attach a cap band to the bottom peg.

5. Connect the second pegs using a single holding band that has been "doubled," or wrapped once on itself.

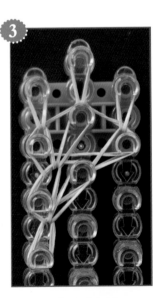

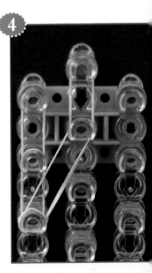

6. Starting from the cap band, loop the bands back to the pegs where they started.

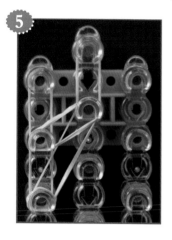

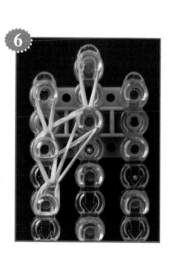

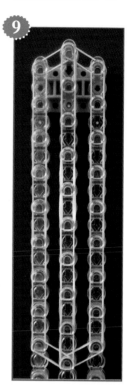

7. To make the eyes, wrap a single black band around your hook several times. To make the whites of the eye, take a single white band and start to wrap it twice around one side of the black bundle, and then finish wrapping on the other side. Repeat this step for the second eye.

8. Slide both eyes onto a single blue band.

9. To make the body of the dolphin, you will be using double bands. Lay out the figure shown, using white bands in the center for the dolphin's belly. Attach the bands on the outside first, followed by the center column.

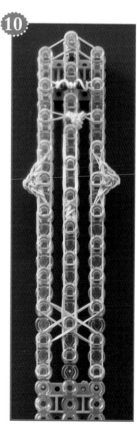

10. Attach the flippers to the outside of the body (from pegs 4, 5, and 6 on both sides). Attach the dorsal fin upside-down from pegs 6 and 7. Attach the eyes and a nose across the face. The nose will just be a single chain with two or three

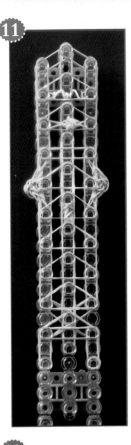

stitches using double bands. At the bottom of the figure, attach two diagonal double bands, and two sets of double bands to the outside columns for the flukes, or the back fin. Finish with a cap band on both.

11. You will now attach holding bands to the body of the dolphin. The top two triangular holding bands will be single bands. The holding band across the fourth row will be a single band that has been "tripled," or wrapped three times on itself. The next two holding bands will be single triangles, followed by two triangular holding bands that have been "doubled" to keep them tight. The final holding band will be a double band, or two bands combined as one.

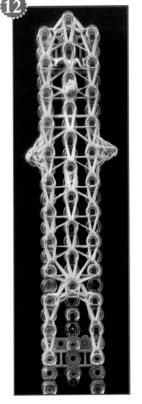

12. Starting from the cap bands, carefully loop all the bands back to the pegs where they started. Loop the outside bands first, then finish with the center column. Secure the top of the project with a c-clip or a rubber band before you take it off the loom.

TULiP

Pretty as a picture, this tulip is so simple and quick that you can make a whole bouquet in no time. These directions are for a small tulip, but if you prefer larger ones, then simply use two rubber bands on every peg, rather than the tight single bands.

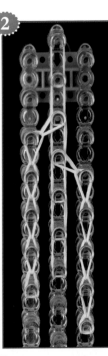

Set up your loom offset so the center column is one peg farther away from you. All bands will be single bands that have been "doubled," or wrapped once on themselves.

1. Using single green bands that have been "doubled," lay out the shape of the stem. Make sure to lay out the center column first, followed by the two outer columns. Tie off the outer leaves with a cap band.

2. Starting from the cap bands in the outside columns, loop the bands back to the pegs where they started until you reach the center stem.

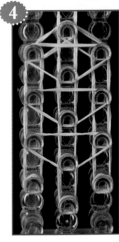

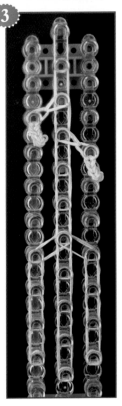

3. Free up the outside columns by detaching the leaves from most of the pegs, but do not remove them completely from the loom. Starting from the end of the stem, lay out the flower shape. Add cap bands to each of the ends of the petals.

4. Add three triangular holding bands to secure the flower. The top triangle will be two pink bands, while the other two will each be single bands that have been "doubled."

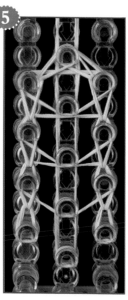

5. Starting from the cap bands, loop the outside columns all the way up to the stem.

6. Next, starting from the cap band in the center column, loop all the bands back to the pegs where they started, continuing all the way up to the top of the stem. Secure the stem with an additional band so the project does not come apart.

7. Carefully remove the project from the loom.

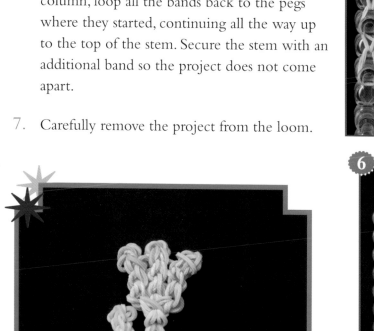

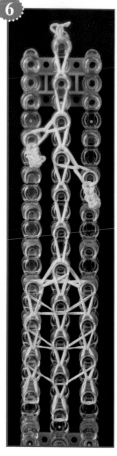

LOCK AND KEY

With this cute little charm, you can show someone special just how you feel about him or her. This makes a fun friendship charm or a gift for a special valentine! Many of these bands are doubled, so be careful when looping!

Difficulty level: **Easy**

You need:

1 loom • 1 hook • yellow bands • red bands • gray bands

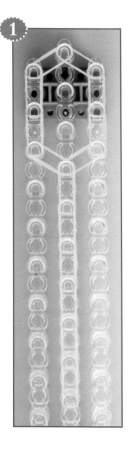

Set up your loom so the center column is one peg away from you.

To Make the Key:

1. Lay down yellow doubled bands in a hexagon shape. Then lay out a line of doubled yellow bands from the fourth to the tenth middle peg.

2. To make the "teeth" of the key, wrap a single yellow band around your hook four times. Then take another single yellow band, double it onto itself, and then thread the looped yellow onto the doubled band. Loop both ends of the band onto the hook. Thread this onto another single yellow band that has been doubled over. Repeat to make two total teeth.

3. To place your "teeth" onto your key, place one onto the last peg, and the second onto the third peg from the end.

4. Loop your key as usual. Secure the final loose loops with a single yellow band pulled into a slipknot.

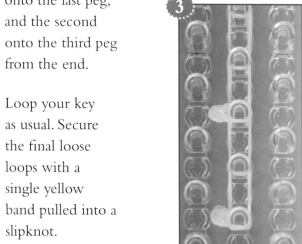

To Make the Lock:

1. Lay a line of doubled yellow bands down the right column until you reach the end. Wrap a single yellow band around the last peg three or four times as a cap band.

2. Loop your yellow chain as usual. Remove from the loom and set aside so that it doesn't unravel.

3. Use double red bands to lay out your lock shape. Attach two red bands from the second middle peg to the first outside peg. Continue laying out double bands to make half a heart shape, then lay out the other half. Wrap a red band around your hook twice and attach it from the second to the third middle peg. Attach two red bands from the third to the fourth middle peg, then attach two gray bands from the fourth to the fifth peg. Wrap a single red band around the last middle peg three or four times as a cap band. Place double red holding bands across the second and third rows. Double the holding band for the fourth row.

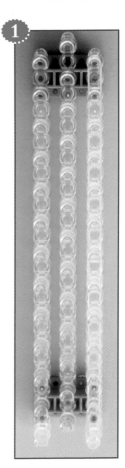

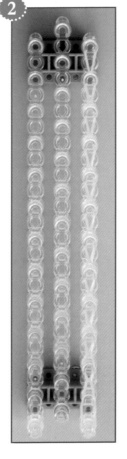

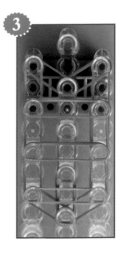

4. Attach your yellow chain from earlier to the first two pegs in the outside columns.

5. Loop your lock as usual. Loop the outside columns first, all the way back to the second middle peg, then loop the middle column. To add more lock detail, wrap a gray band around your hook four times, and when you loop the bands from the fourth to the third peg, thread the looped bands onto the red band before placing it on the peg. Then continue looping as usual. Secure the loose loops with a red band pulled into a slipknot.

SUV

Vrooom! Hit the road with this speedy SUV! Since it uses mostly double bands, this project is sturdier than other projects, making it easy to assemble. Make it in a bunch of colors to make your own gas-guzzling convoy!

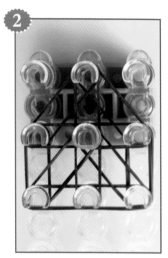

To Make the Wheels:

1. Using double black bands, lay out a pentagon shape, starting at the first and ending on the third middle peg.

2. Attach a single black band to the second middle peg and connect it to the third peg on the right. Continue laying out single bands from the middle peg to the pegs in your pentagon shape, moving in a counterclockwise direction (so you end on the third middle peg). Wrap a red cap band around the middle peg three or four times.

3. Begin looping your "spoke" bands through your cap band and back to the pegs where they started, moving in a clockwise direction (opposite to how you laid them out).

4. Wrap a black cap band around the third middle peg three or four times. Starting at your cap band, begin looping the bands of your pentagon back where they started. Secure the loose loops with a single black band, then remove your wheel from the loom. Repeat to make four total wheels.

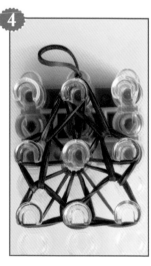

To Make the Windows and Roof:

1. Using clear and red double bands, lay out the shape of your windows and roof. Lay out the clear diagonal bands first: this is your windshield. Then lay out the double clear and red bands down all three columns, as shown.

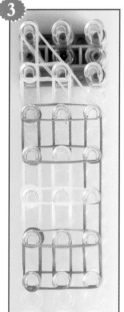

In the seventh row, attach a single red band to each of the outside pegs and connect them to the center peg.

2. Wrap a single band around the second peg in the right column like a cap band, but only wrap it two times. Repeat for the rest of the pegs in the column (skipping the first one). You will use these "connector" bands to attach your car's roof to the body later.

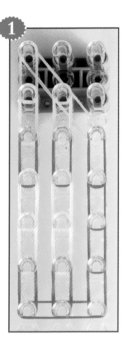

3. Wrap a clear band around your hook twice, then stretch it across the two pegs in the second row. Wrap a red band around your hook twice and place it across all three pegs in the third row. Continue to lay out "holding" bands across the fourth, fifth, and sixth rows, using clear for the fifth row.

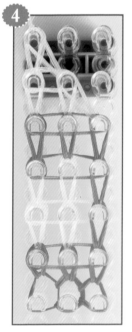

4. Begin looping your shape: start at the last peg in the left column, and loop across the whole row from left to right. Then loop the middle column, followed by the right column. Loop the diagonal clear bands, then finish looping the left column. Secure the loose loops with a single clear band.

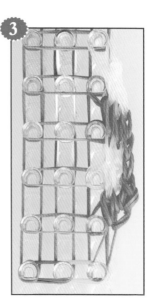

To Make the Car Body:

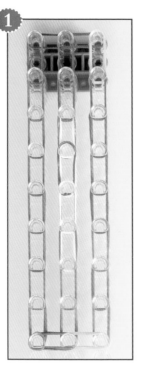

1. Using double bands, lay out the body shape of your car. Wrap a gray cap band around the left peg on the end three or four times.

2. Double a red band and place it across the second to last row in your car shape. Repeat to lay a "holding" band across each row in your car shape, skipping the first and last rows (where your bumpers and lights are).

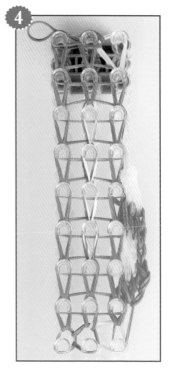

3. Attach your hood and window piece to the loom using the "connector" bands along the outside edge. You will attach it at seven points.

4. Begin looping your car shape, starting on the last peg in the left column, where you placed your cap band. Loop the last row, moving from left to right, then begin looming your right column, where you have attached the top of the SUV. Secure the final loose loops with a single gray band and remove the car from the loom.

5. Use a hook to tuck the end of the gray single band into the car shape. Take up one of your wheel shapes and put your hook through the center. Pull the single black band through the center. Put your hook through your SUV where you would like to put your wheel. Grab the loop from the single black band and pull it through your SUV shape, then open the loop and put the wheel through it to secure it. Put your hook through the same stitch, coming from the side where your wheel is attached, and connect the second wheel to the other side in the same way. Attach the other two wheels.

MONKEY

Go bananas for this monkey project! This fun animal is a great addition to your zoo of charms. Try adding the top hat and making the banana project to make this guy even more fun!

Set up your loom offset so that the center column is one peg farther away from you. All bands are double bands, or two bands combined as one.

1. For the arms, lay out five black double bands. Add two separate cap bands to the bottom of the column—this will make him look like he has fingers.

2. Starting from the cap bands, loop the bands back to the pegs where they started. Secure the bands temporarily, remove it from the loom, and set it aside for later. Repeat these steps for a second arm.

3. This next photo shows how to make both the eyes (left) and the ears (right). For the eyes, attach a single white band, a double black band, and a blue cap band. For the ears, attach a black double band and a cap band.

4. Starting from the cap band, loop the bands back to the pegs where they started. Repeat steps 3 and 4 to make the second eye and ear.

5. For the head of the monkey, lay out the hexagon shape shown in black and white double bands. Make sure to put the bands in the center column on after you have put down the hexagon.

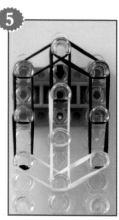

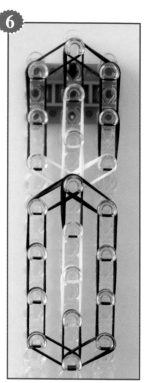

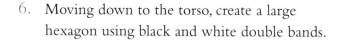

6. Moving down to the torso, create a large hexagon using black and white double bands.

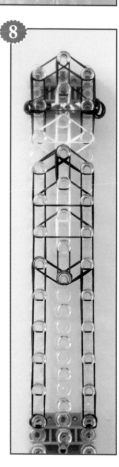

7. Next, attach legs to either side of the monkey. The legs will be five black double bands that are finished off with two separate cap bands on the same peg.

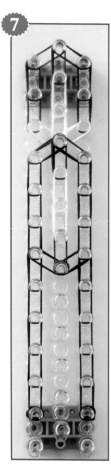

8. Attach two triangular holding bands to the monkey's torso. These are single black bands. Attach the eyes and the ears to the face (both on the second outside pegs), followed by a white and a black holding band.

9. Starting with the feet where you placed your cap bands, begin to loop the bands back to the pegs where they started. Loop the outside columns all the way up

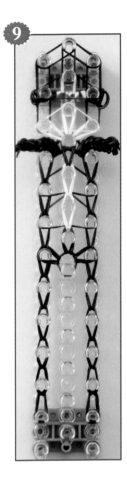

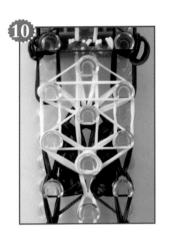

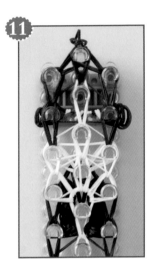

to the tops of the shoulders (the diagonal bands). Here, slide the arms onto the shoulder bands as you are looping them to their pegs. This will keep the arms in place. Do this for both arms, and then loop the center column of the monkey's torso, as well as the white part of his mouth. Stop looping here.

10. Now you will make the big part of the monkey's chin. Push all of the bands and the arms down so they are not in the way, and then start attaching more white bands. First, attach white double bands from the third center peg to the fourth center peg and the from the fourth center peg to the fifth center peg. Take a single white band that has been "doubled" and attach it from pegs 3 to 4 on the left-hand column and another for pegs 3 to 4 in the right-hand column. On each side, take a white double band and attach it diagonally from fourth peg to the fifth center peg. Attach holding bands across the third row, and a single triangular holding band across the fourth row. Attach a cap band to the fifth center peg.

11. Very carefully, loop the rest of these bands back to the top of the monkey's head. Loop the outside columns before the center column, and then secure the project with a rubber band or a c-clip. Gently remove the project from the loom.

SUNGLASSES

Get some shade with these miniature sunglasses! Like the top hat, these sunglasses can be worn by many of our loom creatures. They're also great as a dangling charm for a zipper or necklace! We've chosen to use mostly black bands, but feel free to vary the colors in any way you like.

Difficulty level: **Easy**

You need:

1 loom • 1 hook • black bands • bands in a color of your choice

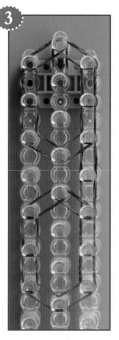

Set up the loom offset so that the center column is one peg farther away from you. All the bands are single bands that have been "doubled," or wrapped once on themselves.

1. First, you will make the sides of the sunglasses. Starting in the right-hand column, lay out a column of "doubled" bands, starting with a bright color and then switching to black. At the eighth peg, connect another "doubled" band diagonally to the center column. Attach a cap band here.

2. From the cap band, loop all the bands back to the pegs where they started, ending at the top of the loom. Secure the top of the project and set aside for later. Repeat these steps for the other side of the sunglasses.

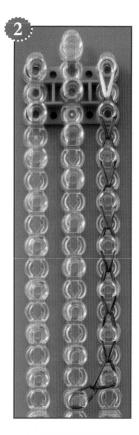

3. Next, turn your loom so that it is horizontal. You will now be laying out the shape of the frames. Using black bands that have been "doubled," or wrapped once on themselves, attach bands to create the shape shown. Note that the single band that has been attached to the center column was laid out before the hexagons in the sunglasses. Make sure to move from left to right when attaching the bands to the loom.

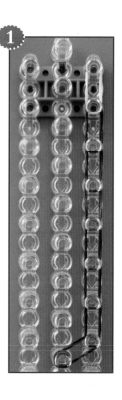

4. Moving from left to right, attach single bands that have been "doubled" to the center columns in both of the sunglass frames.

5. Attach the two sides of the sunglasses to either side of the frames. Also add four triangular holding bands. These are also single bands that have been "doubled."

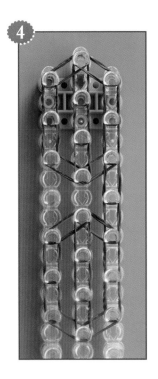

6. Starting from the far right side where you have attached the sides of the glasses, loop your project back. When looping, make sure to loop the far right column (top column if your loom is horizontal) last so that the project stays held together.

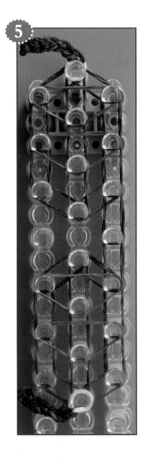

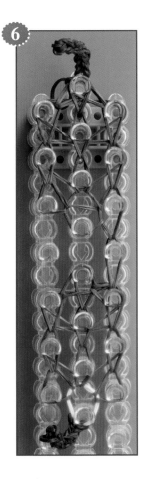

MiTTeNS

Bundle up with your own knitted mittens! Use them as dangly charms to hang from your zipper, add to a bracelet, or attach to earring hooks—these mittens are as cute as can be.

Difficulty level: **Easy**

You need:

1 loom • 1 hook • blue bands • green bands

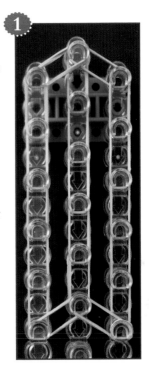

Set up your loom offset so that the center peg is one space farther away from you. All bands are double bands.

1. Lay out your mitten shape, as shown. Notice that the center column has been placed down first, followed by the outer columns. Add your accent colors between pegs 2 and 3 for the outer columns, and between 3 and 4 for the center column.

2. Add three single triangular holding bands to the center of the project and one additional single holding band to the bottom. Note that this last band is a single band that has been "doubled," or wrapped once on itself so that it is taut.

3. For the thumb of your mittens, you will need to do a bit of knitting. Wrap a single band around your hook a few times, and then slide that band onto another double band to create a bundle of bands. Repeat this so you have two bundles as shown in the photo.

4. Using your hooks, slide the outside bands of one bundle onto the outside bands of the other bundle. The piggybacking bands will create the thumb.

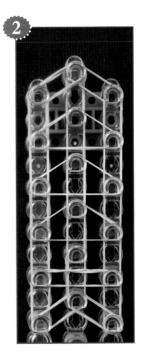

5. Attach the thumb to the loom by the bottom triangular holding band.

6. Loop the project back to the pegs where they started. Make sure to loop the pegs in the center column last.

7. Tie the project off with a rubber band at the top and carefully remove from the loom. Repeat each of these steps for a second mitten.

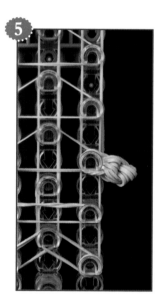

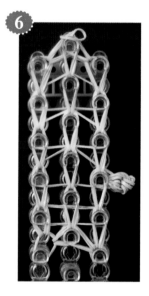

MiGHTY SWORD

Carry a sword like the greatest knights! Luckily, your limbs are safe since the sword is made of rubber. We have added bands to look like gemstones in the hilt of the sword, but feel free to add them wherever you like, or even use real beads. This project is quite simple, but can get tricky when knitting the gems. For extra tips on how to knit, see the glossary at the beginning of the book.

Difficulty level: **Medium**

You need:

1 loom • 2 hooks • gray bands • green bands • blue bands • orange bands

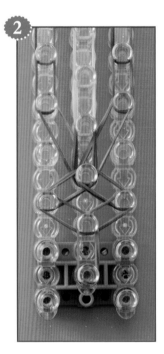

Set up your loom offset so that the center column is one peg further away from you.

1. Using double bands (two bands combined as one), lay out the blade of the sword. Start by placing the bands in the center column first, stopping at the tenth peg down, then attaching the outer columns. Leave a gap between the last band in the center column and the peg where the outer columns connect to the eleventh center peg. Note that all the diagonal bands stretch farther than normal.

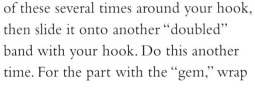

2. Using a gray band, connect the gap in your sword to the peg below where the diagonal bands attach. Next, add gray double bands in a diamond shape to create the center of the guard. Attach an additional gray double band to the last peg in the center column and close it off with a cap band.

3. For the guard of the sword (the two sides that stem outward), you will need to do a little knitting. Start by creating a single chain of lime green bands using single bands that have been "doubled," or wrapped once on themselves. Wrap one of these several times around your hook, then slide it onto another "doubled" band with your hook. Do this another time. For the part with the "gem," wrap

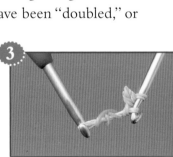

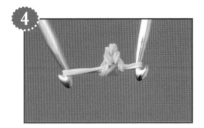

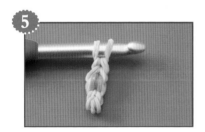

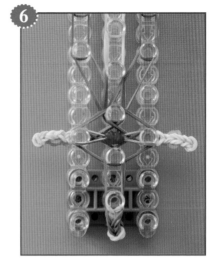

an orange band several times around a second hook and slide it onto another doubled band. Connect this to the bundle you already have by attaching the band with the gem to the first hook, and then sliding one side of the first bundle onto the band with the gem.

4. Remove the side of the band (from the original bundle) that is not connected to the band with the gem, and reattach it to the opposite side of the band with the gem. (You will need to hold the band with the gem with your finger or a hook while you do this.) Your bands should now appear on either side of the orange gem.

5. Finish the rest of this side of the guard of the sword as a normal single chain by adding two more sets of bands. Repeat steps 3 through 5 for a second side of the guard.

6. Attach the guard of the sword to the diamond shape you created. For the gem in the center, simply wrap a blue band around a hook several times and slide it onto a gray double band, attaching the gray band to the sword. For the grip of the sword, repeat the same process as the guard (steps 3 through 5), but vary your colors.

7. Attach eight holding bands to the blade of the sword to hold it together. All these are single bands that have been "doubled," or wrapped once on themselves.

8. Starting from the pommel, or the tip of the handle where you've placed a cap band, loop your band back to the pegs where they started. When you're looping the blade of the sword, loop the outside columns first, and then finish by looping the center column all the way to the top. Secure the top of the project with a band or a c-clip.

HAPPY HiPPO

King of the river, this hippopotamus is all sorts of fun! This project has a lot of little steps and attachments, so make sure to pay close attention to each. Once you're finished, you'll have one of the coolest animals to add to your loom kingdom!

Difficulty level: **Medium**

You need:

1 loom • 2 hooks • c-clips (optional) • white bands • black bands (or other eye color) • purple rubber bands

Set up your loom offset, with the center column set one peg away from you.

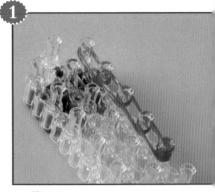

1. Starting with the front legs of the hippo, lay out four purple triple bands. Instead of a regular cap band, you will add three separate cap bands to the last peg to make an extra strong cap band.

2. Loop your bands back to the pegs where they started. Secure the end of the leg with a c-clip, or slide it onto a holding hook temporarily. You will use the leg later.

3. Repeat steps 1 and 2 for the second front leg and set aside.

4. Repeat step 1. This time, though, add an additional triple band between the second and third pegs down in the center column.

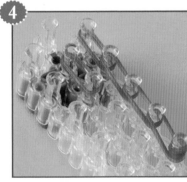

5. Loop your bands back to the pegs where they started, with one exception: when you reach the middle peg in the column, loop the band over to the lone triple band in the center column, then loop this band. Return to the right-hand column and loop the last band, as shown.

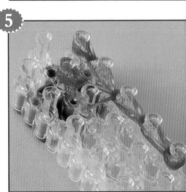

6. Secure the ends with a c-clip or slide the project onto a hook temporarily. Make sure both top loops are secured before removing from the loom. Repeat steps 4 and 5 to make the second hind leg and set aside with the other legs.

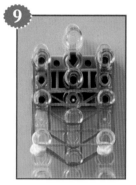

7. To make the hippo's bottom jaw, lay out a pattern of purple double bands, as shown. Note that the first sets of diagonal bands (that go from the second outside pegs to connect to the third center peg) are single bands. The double band that goes from the third to the fourth center pegs should be attached last.

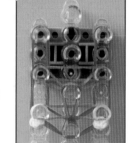

8. To make the bottom teeth, you will make a very short single chain. To do this, wrap a white double band around a hook three times. Attach another white double band to the hook, and slide the first bundle onto it. Reattach the other end of the double bands to create the tooth. Make two and set aside, as shown. For smaller teeth, use single bands.

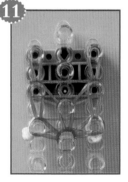

9. Attach the teeth to the jaw you created. To secure, lay out two holding bands. These are single bands that have been wrapped once on themselves so that they stretch tightly across the loom.

10. Loop the bottom center bands and the diagonal bands back to the pegs where they started, as shown.

11. After, start back at the bottom of your figure and loop the bottom diagonal bands as well as the outside columns. The holding bands stay where they are.

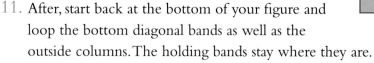

12. Secure this figure with c-clips or by sliding it onto a hook and set aside temporarily.

13. The next figure is the hippo's upper jaw. Lay out the figure shown using purple double bands, starting with the outside columns and then the center column.

14. Repeat step 8 to make the upper teeth. Make two nostrils this same way using single purple bands, but slide these onto a single band that has been wrapped once on itself (making it taut).

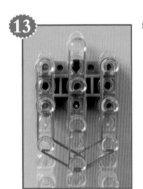
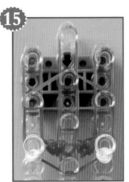
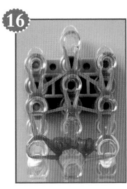
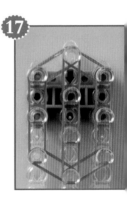

15. Attach the teeth to the figure. To attach the nostrils, stretch the single band holding the nostrils across the loom to connect to the outer columns. Lay out a single holding band in a triangular shape close to the top of the figure.

16. Loop the bands back to the pegs where they started. Begin with the center column, and then move to the outside columns. Secure the top of the project and remove from the loom. You will attach this to the hippo's body later.

17. For the hippo's head, lay out the figure shown using purple double bands. Attach the outside columns first, followed by the center column.

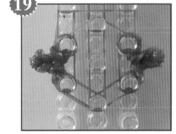

18. For the rest of his body, attach purple double bands for the outer shape. For the center column, use purple triple bands for each of the bands except the last (this will be a double band). The triple bands will make his body bigger.

19. Lay out three double holding bands over the body of the hippo—each will form a triangle. Take the hind legs that you made earlier and attach them to the bottom of the figure. Since there are two loops at the top of each leg, you will use these loops to stretch across two pegs.

20. When you start looping the body back, start with only the outside columns and very bottom peg in the center column. Loop only to the top of the torso, and do not loop the diagonal bands just yet.

21. To attach the front legs, you will begin as if you are looping the diagonal bands back to the pegs where they started. Before attaching the bands to their original peg, though, slide the leg onto the band, and then attach the band to the peg.

22. Before you loop the hippo's head, you will attach holding bands, ears, and the eyes. Both the ears and the eyes will be made in just the same

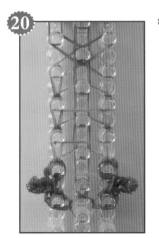

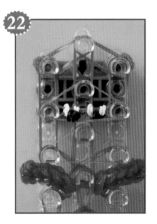

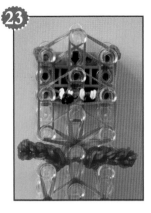

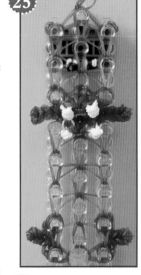

way as the teeth, except you will use different colors. For the eyes, use a single black band and two white bands, and for the ears, use single purple bands. Slide the eyes onto a single purple band and attach this across his face. Attach two single holding bands in triangular shapes over his face, as shown.

23. Next, carefully loop the bottom three bands on the hippo's face, as shown.

24. Attach the bottom of the hippo's jaw to the same area. Push the bands down as far as possible so they don't pop off the loom.

25. Then attach the top of the hippo's mouth to the same area. Since there are three loops that need to attach to the loom, it's easiest to place one section down and loop the bands back to the peg where it started, securing this section of the mouth. Notice how the areas where the mouth is attached are looped back in the photo.

26. Finish looping the rest of the head and secure the top of the hippo's head with a c-clip or a purple double band.

27. Carefully remove the project from the loom. If you'd like to add a tail, create a small chain and attach it to his hindquarters.

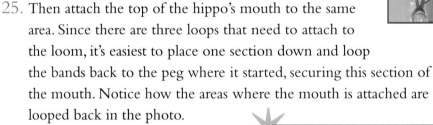

SKUNK

This stinker's quick to put together, and he's awfully sweet.
His leg bands are doubled, so remember to loop carefully!

Difficulty level: **Easy**

You need:

1 loom • 1 hook • black bands • white bands • blue bands

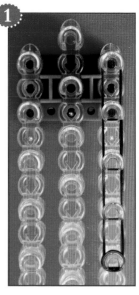

To Make the Legs:

1. Lay down a line of doubled black bands from the first to the fifth peg. Wrap a single black band around the fifth peg three or four times as a cap band.

2. Loop your black bands back. Remove your chain from the loom and set aside. Repeat to make four total legs.

To Make the Tail:

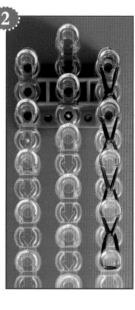

1. Attach two black bands from the first to the second middle peg. Using white single bands, lay out a long hexagon, starting on the second and ending on the seventh middle peg. Lay bands down the middle of your hexagon shape: start with double bands, then three bands from the

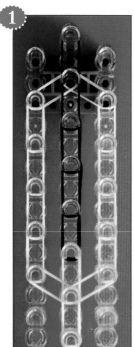

third to the fourth, then finish with two more sets of double black, then double white bands for the last peg. Attach double white bands from the seventh to the eighth middle peg, then wrap a white band around the eighth middle peg three or four times as a cap band.

2. Place "holding bands" across your shape by doubling bands and placing them onto the loom in a triangle shape. Repeat to lay four total holding bands up your tail shape.

3. Loop your tail, remove it from the loom, and set aside. Secure the loose loops with your hook or a temporary slip knot to keep it from unraveling.

To Make the Body:

1. Lay down a line of double bands from the first to the fourth middle peg: use white for the first two sets, then switch to black. Using black double bands, lay out a hexagon shape.

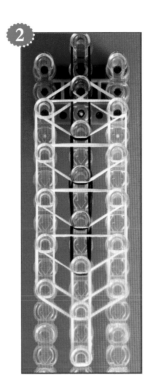

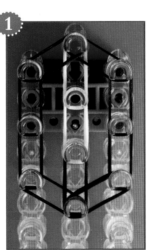

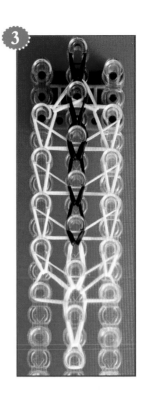

2. Starting at the fourth middle peg and using double black bands, lay out another larger hexagon shape. Lay a line of bands down the center of your larger hexagon: start with two black bands, then switch to double white bands.

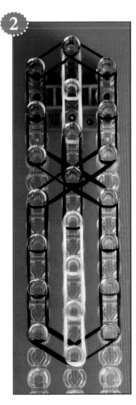

3. To make the eyes, wrap a blue band around your hook four times, then take a single white band and wrap it around the hook four times, so that there are two white loops on either side of the blue band. Repeat to make the second eye on your hook. Then thread both eye pieces onto a single black band. Place it across the second row.

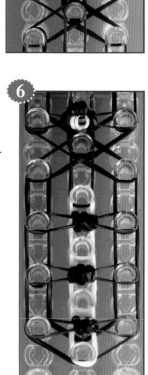

4. To make the snout, wrap a black band around your hook four times, then thread it onto double black bands. Before looping the end of the double black bands back onto your hook, loop a white band three times around the hook. Thread the black and white bands onto a single black band. Set aside, or look ahead to attach your snout to the third row on the loom.

5. To make the ears, wrap a single black band around your hook four times, then thread it onto a single black band doubled over. Repeat to make two ears. Place your ears onto the loom on the first pegs in the outside columns.

6. To make black stripes for your skunk's back, take two black bands and wrap them around your hook three times, then thread them onto a single black band. Place the stripe across the fifth row. Repeat twice more to place three total stripes down your skunk's back.

7. Attach your skunk's tail to the last center peg, and his back legs to the last outside pegs.

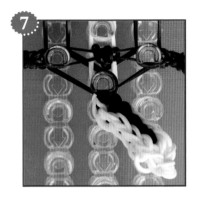

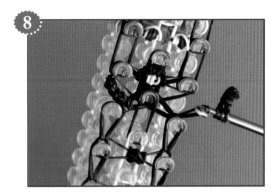

8. Begin looping your skunk shape. Loop the first center peg, then loop up the outside columns until you reach the "shoulder" pegs. To attach the front legs, place a leg on your hook, then when looping the outside peg to the neck peg, thread the leg onto the band before placing it onto the neck peg.

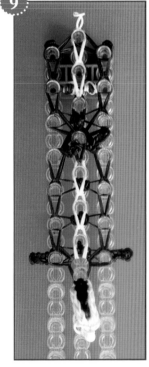

9. Loop up the middle pegs of your skunk's back, then continue looping the skunk shape as usual. Secure the loose loops with a single band pulled into a slip knot.

DRAGONFLY

Fly away with this fun project! Try using glow-in-the-dark bands for the wings for an extra cool dragonfly that lights up at night!

Difficulty level: **Medium**

You need:

1 loom • 1 hook • clear green bands • blue bands • teal bands • lime green bands • black bands • pink bands

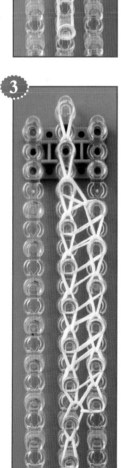

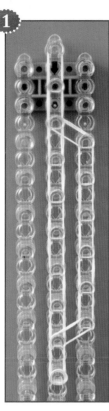

Set up your loom offset so that the center column is one peg farther away from you.

1. For the wings, lay out the figure shown, starting with the center column and then branching out to the right-hand column. These will be single bands that have been "doubled," or wrapped once on themselves. Attach a cap band at the bottom of the figure.

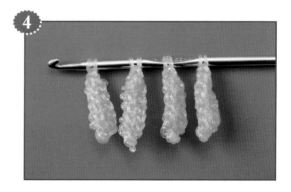

2. Attach five holding bands to secure the wing. These are single bands that have been "doubled."

3. Starting from the cap band at the bottom of the wing, loop the bands back to the pegs where they started until you reach the top of the wing.

4. Repeat these steps to create four total wings.

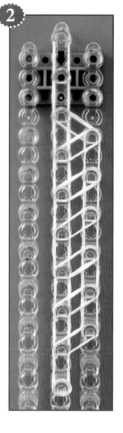

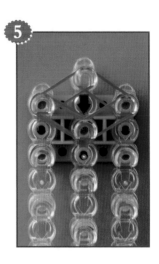

5. Using blue bands, create the head of the dragonfly. These will be double bands, or two bands that are used at the same time.

6. Place a teal double band down the center of the head. Create a hexagon shape for the thorax (the next part of the body) using teal double bands.

7. Attach two double bands down the center of the body.

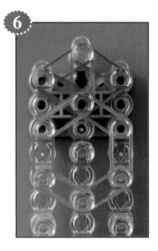

8. At the bottom of the thorax, lay out the long part of the abdomen using double bands for seven rows. We alternated using pink, teal, and blue colors, but you can use whatever colors you like. Attach a cap band at the bottom of the project.

9. To create the eyes, take a black band, a blue band, and a lime green band and wrap them several times around your hook. Do this again for a second eye, and then slide them onto a single blue band.

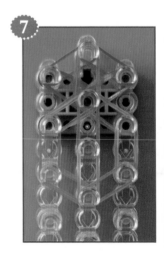

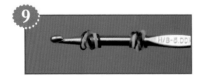

10. Stretch this single band to attach the eyes to the top outside pegs in the head. Attach a single teal holding band to the thorax to hold the project in place.

11. Connect the four wings to the four pegs in the thorax, as shown.

12. Starting with the bottom of the dragonfly, loop the bands back up all the way to the top of the dragonfly's head. Be careful not to skip bands or go out of order. Attach two rubber bands to the top of the project to secure it. These can also be the dragonfly's antennae.

LiON

Get ready to roar with your loom lion! This king of the jungle requires a lot of bands for his mane, so just be careful when you are looping the project back to keep all of them secure. We chose orange and yellow bands for this project, but you can try out different shades, or even make his mane rainbow-colored!

Difficulty level: **Medium**

You need:

1 loom • 2 hooks • yellow bands • orange bands • black bands • white bands

Set up your loom offset so that the center column is one peg farther away from you. All bands will be double bands.

1. To make the legs, you will set up a single chain on your loom. Lay out four yellow double bands and finish with a cap band on the last peg.

2. Starting from the cap band, loop the bands back to the pegs where they started. Secure the top of the leg on a holding hook or with a temporary c-clip and set aside. Repeat steps 1 and 2 for the second leg.

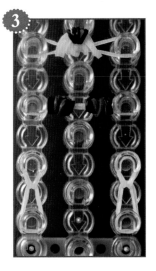

3. Next you will create the nose, eyes, and ears. For the nose, wrap a yellow double band around your hook several times. Slide this onto a single yellow band to create a small bundle. Wrap a single black band around your hook several times. Slide this onto a yellow double band. Slide this bundle onto the first bundle—you will need to switch between hooks as if you are knitting. For the eyes, wrap a single blue band around your hook several times, then wrap the first half of a black band on one side of

the blue band, and then finish on the other. Repeat this for the second eye and then slide both eyes onto a single yellow band. For the ears, attach a single yellow band to your loom and finish it with a cap band. Loop this band back to its original peg. Set all these aside for later.

4. To make the lion's head and mane, you will create a hexagon of yellow double bands, as shown in the photo. Before attaching the bands to the loom, slide five or six orange bands over the yellow bands, then attach the yellow bands to the loom.

5. In the center of the mane, attach two more bands down the center column. These bands will also have five or six orange bands over them as well before you attach them to the loom.

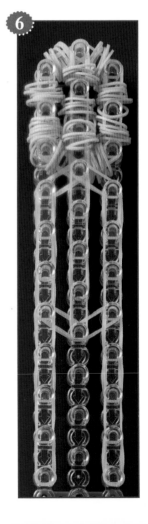

6. To make the body of the lion, attach a large hexagon to your loom, but continue down four additional pegs on the outside columns for the legs. Finish those columns with cap bands. Fill in the center of the belly *after* you have laid out the hexagon of the lion's belly. If you'd like, switch to orange bands in the center of the lion's torso. Place a cap band at the bottom peg in the center column where the torso ends.

7. Attach the ears to the first pegs in the outside columns, attach the eyes to the second pegs in the outside columns, and attach the nose to the third pegs in the outside columns. Attach two

triangular holding bands to the center of the lion's belly.

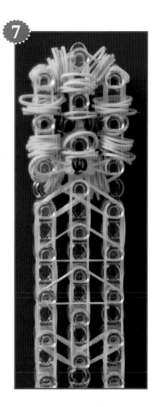

8. On the second and third outside pegs, add four or five more orange bands for the mane, and hold them in place with triangular holding bands, as shown.

9. Starting from the cap bands at the bottom of the legs, begin to loop your project back to the pegs where they started. Loop the outside columns first until you reach the shoulder bands, or just before the mane starts. As you are looping these diagonal bands, slide the arms onto the bands and finish looping it onto the center peg. Loop the center column of the belly up to the peg just before the mane to secure everything.

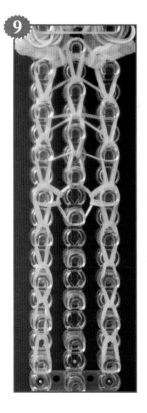

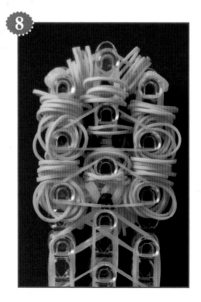

10. Carefully loop the face and mane back. There are a lot of bands, so you may need to use another hook to fish your way to the bands that need to be looped. Loop the outside columns before the center column, and add additional orange bands to the three pegs at the top to make the mane bigger.

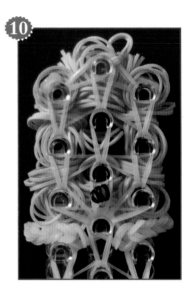